Towards the Light

To Joyce

Where noted, names and places in this book
have been changed to protect individuals'
identity and preserve their privacy.

The cover is adapted from a painting by Joyce
Compere. It currently resides in the collection of
Doug and Tanya Mark

ISBN 0-9777235-9-3
978-0-9777235-9-1
All Rights Reserved
Copyright © 2010 by John S. Compere

First Printing, November 2010
Trade Paperback Edition

Printed in the United States of America
Writers Cramp Publishers
http://www.writerscramp.us/
editor@writerscramp.us

Towards the Light

A Fifth Generation Baptist Minister's Journey from Religion to Reason

John S. Compere, Ph. D.

PROLOGUE

I have many interests, but one consuming passion: what can we do about the problem religion poses for today's world?

Religion is not just a footnote to today's history. It is the key player in the drama -- the tragedy -- that is unfolding between the developed Western world and the world of Islam. Unless we find a way to solve the dilemma that religion poses for our world, none of us may live to see a 22nd century.

The emotional, bronze-age theology which energizes both sides in the current conflict, combined with the highly-sophisticated nuclear technology of our time, may bring on a holocaust from which there is no escape.

Essentially all syndicated columnists in the U.S.A. eschew any serious criticism of the ideology associated with any religion. My guess is that the reluctance to criticize religious beliefs comes from the assumption that we need to be sensitive to all belief systems, which are emotionally-based by definition and not amenable to logical investigation. However, that leaves many of us in the educated world in a position similar to having to act as if we think a belief in fairies deserves respect. If the belief, or lack of belief, in fairies were so contentious that whole groups of people were murdering those on the other side who believed in a different kind of fairy, wouldn't it make sense to point out that there is absolutely no evidence that fairies exist and that to kill one another over the issue is insane?

The reality is that religious belief systems are accorded a kind of respect entirely out of proportion to their evidence or logical justification. At some point, intelligent, educated people need to be urged to use their reasoning faculties to question whether their religious systems can stand up to logical analysis.

I did not have much choice but to engage in this kind of investigation. As the story of my pilgrimage from Baptist minister to atheist will reveal, religion was my life from the earliest time I can remember. I imbibed it, learned it, believed it, and lived it 24/7. It came naturally to me as a caring human being to want to give my life to making the world a better place, and since I assumed, due to my upbringing, that religion was the avenue for accomplishing that, becoming anything but a minister was not an option I even considered.

However, because I also had a scientific, investigative mind-set, I could not help beginning to question the tenets I had been taught. I tried not to, because doing so called into doubt everything my life stood for. But I couldn't stop the process once it had begun.

It wasn't an easy or quick re-orientation. Instead, it was agonizingly, painfully slow. As I look back on it now, I wonder how I could have ever believed any of the basic tenets of Christianity -- they appear so patently absurd -- but there was not much way to speed up the growth process. Just as physical and psychological growth occurs slowly in the main, with short bursts of growth interspersed in the gradual process, so growth in understanding what life is about takes time. And if you have imbibed deeply in the pervasive religious assumptions of your culture, it isn't easy to break free. When I was growing up, I literally could not imagine what it would be like not to have religion as the most important thing in my life.

This is why I talk about the metamorphosis I went through as "outgrowing" religion.

I know that the idea that religion needs to be outgrown will be terribly offensive to religion's true believers. And I want to reassure such people, if any of them choose to actually read this work, that if your religious faith is working just fine for you -- which means not only that it gives you comfort and a sense of belonging you don't find anywhere else, but also that it makes you more accepting, more understanding, more humane, in short a kinder, gentler person -- by all means continue in your faith without worrying that someone like me had to become an atheist in order to maintain any sort of integrity.

But I'm persuaded that millions of people have encountered doubts about religion's authenticity, just as I did, and will welcome some help in being able to allow themselves to openly outgrow all religious ideology, just as we allow our children to outgrow belief in Santa and the Easter bunny.

I'm further persuaded that if a significant number of such people begin to see the world from a humanistic perspective and quit believing in such things as prayer, an afterlife, the need for forgiveness for being human, our world will be much, much better off, and humanity may even survive to create a more humane world for future generations.

I need to note that although most of the specific criticisms against religion I make in this book are from my lifetime of experience in the world of protestant Christianity, I know enough about other religions to be convinced that adherence to them is also problematic since they suffer from the same lack of evidence for their accuracy.

The sooner the bulk of humanity comes to terms with the reality that what each of us has is one life, stretching only until we breathe our last breath, and begin putting our energies into making the one life that each of us has as meaningful and rewarding as possible, the better off the world will be.

To paraphrase a Biblical phrase: even so come, secular humanism.

Even so, come.

FROM BAPTIST MINISTER TO ATHEIST

I can't begin to remember when I first started believing in the teachings of the church, but I remember the precise moment when I became aware of my first doubts.

I was a sophomore in college, already an ordained minister of the Southern Baptist variety, and was preparing to deliver a sermon in one of the larger Baptist Churches in Mississippi, the state where I was born and bred. I had gotten another college student to fill in for me in the pulpit of the small, country church of which I was the minister, and to which I drove from my college campus every weekend to preach, so that I could accept the invitation to fill the pulpit for one Sunday in a very prestigious First Baptist Church of which a friend of my father's was the minister.

I was very excited at this opportunity to "strut my stuff" before this large congregation and had worked very hard at preparing my best sermon for delivery on this momentous occasion. When I arrived at the church, I was ushered into the pastor's study and graciously left alone for some quiet time before the eleven o'clock worship service began. As was my wont, I was soon pacing back and forth quietly practicing the sermon I was soon to deliver by actually saying the words out loud to myself.

It was going very well until I found myself saying something about the eternal punishment which awaited those who refused to believe in Jesus, standard protestant fare. All of a sudden, quite unbidden, a thought intruded on my mind. "Is that really true? Could it possibly be that everyone who hasn't trusted in Jesus is doomed to spend eternity burning in hell? Even all those billions of people who live in distant lands and have been raised in other religious traditions?" I know it seems strange that I was just then asking this question, which every intelligent believer has asked throughout the centuries, but it will begin to make sense when you've heard my whole story.

Anyway, I was thunderstruck by this unwanted thought and quite taken aback by the audacity of it. How dare such a thought intrude on my preparation for this big ministerial moment! I pushed the thought aside as best I could and continued with my pulpit preparation. I delivered the morning sermon with as much aplomb as I could muster, stayed in one of the member's homes for the afternoon, being treated as if I were someone special, and then went back to the church that night to deliver another sermon for the evening service. Then I got in my car to drive back to the college campus.

No sooner had I gotten behind the wheel than the doubts about this horrible doctrine of eternal punishment for all non-believers began again in earnest. Big time!

There was no use trying to stop the thoughts. If

this basic doctrine of the faith concerning the existence of hell were not true, which, once I had begun to think about it, I knew absolutely had to be the case, what else about what I had always believed might not be true as well. It was as if a dam had burst in my mind, letting loose the flood waters of critical doubt about the authenticity of the Christian faith, and I was treading water mightily to try to stay afloat.

I know that to people who were raised in a more normal situation, where religion was either just an accepted thing, but no big, huge deal, or in a home where one was free to believe or not believe, it must seem strange that I found these doubts about the faith I had been taught so disturbing.

What's the big deal? Why not just accept that I had concluded that I didn't believe what I had been taught, as millions of other people do, and choose another profession so I could get on with my life. After all, I was only eighteen. Plenty of time to change my college major, prepare for another career, and move on out.

Well, I simply wasn't able to do that at that time. The reason has to do with my life story up until that point. So let's go back a few years.

I was the third child born into the home of a Southern Baptist minister and his wife. My mother was as much a minister, though not in name or salary, as my father.

My father was fourth generation minister. That meant, of course, that when I was ordained as a minister at age 18, I was the latest of five generations of ministers in my immediate family.

My great, great grandfather, Lee Compere, and his wife Susanna had come to these shores in 1820 under the auspices of the London Missionary Society as missionaries to Native Americans. The couple had earlier gone to Jamaica as missionaries, where they were instrumental in establishing what was to become the First Baptist Church of Kingston. After less than two years in Jamaica, Lee contracted malaria, from which he couldn't seem to recover, and was given medical advice that he needed either to return to the cooler clime of England or move on to America.

Because they were so convinced that they were meant to be missionaries, the young couple decided to come on to America rather than return to England. Aboard a wooden sailing ship on the sea voyage to this country their first child, an infant daughter, contracted a high fever and died within a few hours. Imagine the heartbreak the young parents felt as they wrapped the tiny body in a blanket, dropped it over the side of the ship and watched it slip beneath the cold waves of the Atlantic Ocean!

By the time the couple landed in Charleston, SC, they were a haggard and distraught pair, but their faith in God and in their calling to be His missionaries had not wavered. They lived for a time in the home of the Rev. Richard Furman, minister of the First Baptist Church of Charleston, SC, for whom Furman University was named, and soon moved out to live among the Creek Indians to continue their missionary work.

As the US government moved the Native Americans westward, my great, great grandparents moved with them, establishing churches like the First Baptist Church of Montgomery, AL, and state associations of Baptist churches along the way in Georgia, Alabama, and Mississippi. They moved on through Arkansas and Oklahoma, with Lee eventually dying in Texas.

A book by one of my distant cousins written for use in mission study groups in Southern Baptist churches suggests that the longer they lived with the Creek Indians, the more they came to respect them and their traditions and the less emphasis they placed on the number of them they were able to baptize into the faith. This became such a problem that the London Missionary Society began to question their ministry and eventually cut off all financial support.

It didn't matter to Lee and Susanna. They continued their ministry to these people who were being systematically mistreated by the government, living among them and teaching their children how to read and write. They also learned the Creek language, and Lee succeeded in translating significant portions of the Bible into the Creek language.

Lee and Susanna, who were known as abolitionists, were strongly opposed to the institution of slavery. However, it was a strange anomaly that the Creeks, who were being so badly treated by the US government, were also slave owners. The Creeks made it known that they did not want their slaves to be exposed to the Christian gospel, but Lee and Susanna continued to invite them to religious services.

On one occasion while Lee was away preaching in another community and Susanna was holding services in which slaves were present, some Creek tribesmen stormed the sanctuary, dragged the slaves out into the churchyard and proceeded to torture and beat them.

This horrible event spelled the beginning of the end of the missionaries' work with the Creeks.

This missionary couple was clearly genuinely sincere in their faith, approaching their ministry in an unassuming way which only wanted to help better the lives of those to whom they felt called to minister. They were, according to reports written in Baptist annals of the time, capable and caring people.

I won't bore you with more details except to say that at the time of the death of my great, great grandfather, all three of his sons were ministers, two of his four daughters had married ministers, and all seven of his children were strong supporters of the Baptist churches of which they were members.

One of Lee and Susanna's minister sons was my great grandfather, William Samuel Compere, who ended up staying in Mississippi, teaching in the largest Baptist college in the state, Mississippi College (from which I also graduated), and serving various churches in the area.

Then came my grandfather, Ebenezer John Compere, who was also a minister and who died from a fall off a ladder while helping a church member erect a barn. My father was just a small boy when his father died, so I never knew my paternal grandfather. My father's mother was a schoolteacher, a well-meaning, but stern, woman who had one consuming mission in life: find out who's to blame, and blame 'em!

Much of the time when I lived with her briefly in the first grade, I was the one to blame! I was not a particularly bad kid. I was just full of energy and inquisitiveness, and my grandmother had zero tolerance for any sort of mischief, no matter how minor.

My father and mother, William Lowrey and Jacqueline Senter Compere, met when they were both nominated for the post of president of the Mississippi Baptist Student Union when they were college students. My dad was a student at Mississippi College, studying for the Baptist ministry and my mother was a student at another Baptist college in Mississippi, Blue Mountain College, an all-girls school at the time. As I mentioned earlier, her family was also very, very religious, with her father establishing a church on his own property and filling the pulpit on many occasions, even though he was a dentist by profession. His wife, my grandmother, played the pump organ and sang solos. One of my mother's brothers was a minister, and all of her siblings were leaders in the Baptist churches of which they were members.

My mother had wanted to be a missionary herself, but when she married my father, she contented herself with being the best minister's wife she could be. She played the piano in the church, taught Sunday School classes, sang in the choir, and spent most of her time trying to make sure my dad's influence as a minister was in good shape. She was as much of a minister as any of the men who were formally ordained to do this work (Baptists refer to it as a "calling"), but of course in those days it was only males who were considered for ordination. She had a double major in English and speech from college and was actually better in the pulpit than my father, though she worked very hard to be sure he was the one who got most of the attention. A product of her time, she made it a point to say that she was not a "women's libber" when the feminist movement came along in the 1960's.

The life of our family was completely oriented around the church. My brother, sister, and I were adjuncts to my father's ministry. We went to every church meeting there was, without fail. On Sunday mornings, we weren't allowed to read the newspaper because we were supposed to be reading our Sunday

School lessons or otherwise getting ready for church. I can remember dashing home as soon as I could after church so that I could get to the newspaper. As soon as the whole family got home, we all helped prepare lunch. It wasn't until the dishes were done that I was allowed to go out to play with my friends, but not for long since there were church services that evening as well.

All three of us children sang in church choirs, first youth choirs, then adult choirs before we were really adults. We all learned to play musical instruments -- my brother played the marimba, my sister played the violin, and I played the clarinet. Our family entertainment consisted of gathering around the piano, playing and singing, almost exclusively religious songs, of course.

The church was not just a part of my life in my family of origin; it was my whole life!

Everything we did was oriented around the church and its teachings. One of the teachings which impacted me significantly was the idea that our purpose here on this earth, our goal in life, is to glorify God. That means that you don't do what you would like to do; you do what you must. You cannot strive for success, however worthy the cause. You must only strive to please God.

I was ten years of age when I officially became a Christian and was baptized into church membership. In that church tradition an invitation to join the church is issued at the end of every service, both for those who are not yet baptized and are now ready to "accept Jesus as savior", as well as for people who are already members of other Baptist churches who want to transfer their membership to the local congregation.

The invitation is given, an appropriate "invitation hymn" is sung, and people have to come to the front of the church to shake the minister's hand and make public their request for membership. The congregation then votes to accept them into the "fellowship of believers".

No one talked to me about becoming a Christian, formally joining the church and being baptized. It just dawned on me during one Sunday service that I hadn't done that yet, and I proceeded to walk down the aisle as the invitation hymn was being sung to shake my father's hand and to say that I was "accepting Jesus as my savior". This experience was supposed to be accompanied by my repenting of my sins, but I had honestly not had a chance to do much sinning! About the worst thing I had done to date was talk with my buds during the church service, which was usually accompanied by my father stopping in the middle of his sermon to glare at me for what seemed like an eternity and felt like the end of the world at the time. Whenever this occurred, I just knew that when we got home, I'd get a severe "lecture" on how disrespectful I had been, how much I had hurt my father, to say nothing of offending God, by my inappropriate talking in church. This was generally followed by a whipping with a switch from a tree in the yard. I was usually relieved when the actual switching began because that meant the shaming lecture was over!

I could stand the pain better than the shame!

It was only a couple of years later that it became clear that I was destined for the ministry. I discovered that I had a knack for holding people's attention when I spoke in public, which I did often in various youth groups at the church. I remember going to a huge public rally on a Saturday night at the city auditorium in Jackson to hear a well-known Baptist preacher named R. G. Lee deliver a sermon for which he was famous in church circles. The sermon was called "Payday Someday." It was a dramatic presentation which began with the story of King Ahab and Queen Jezebel and talked in very graphic terms about how the punishment for rebellion against God was a certainty. The next morning in my Sunday School class, I began to tell my classmates about the experience of the night before and found myself able to quote much of Dr. Lee's sermon verbatim. They encouraged me, so I continued for most of the class period. I heard later that all the other classes in that part of the church stopped their lessons to listen to my delivery of "Payday Someday," which I'm sure I did at the top of my lungs. My parents began to hear from church members that I would surely follow in my father's ministerial footsteps. Soon I had gone down to the front of the church to make known my intention of "surrendering" to the call to the ministry.

As I look back on it now, I realize that I didn't really have a choice. I was destined to be a minister from the day I took my first breath. Ministry was in my genes, in my familial history, and everyone who knew me expected me to become a minister.

I preached my first formal sermon when I was 15. It got rave reviews from the congregation at my father's church, not because the sermon was that good -- I'm sure it wasn't very good at all because I had no idea how to prepare a sermon -- but because I was so young and had an inherited ability to feel comfortable with public speaking. Although a penchant for public speaking clearly was a genetic inheritance from my father's side of the family, I actually think that my mother's genes contributed more to my comfort in the pulpit than did my father's. One of her sisters, my favorite aunt, was one of the most delightful storytellers I've ever known. I learned early on that the way to hold the attention of an audience is with a good story.

I heard plenty of good stories during my youth, but all of them were religious in nature. I just assumed that this was the way the world was. It was only after I became an adult that I realized how different things in my family were from the growing-up experience of most people.

For instance, we essentially did not celebrate birthdays in our home. I never once had a birthday party or birthday cake, nor did either of my siblings to my knowledge. My parents didn't celebrate their own birthdays and certainly didn't take the children to buy a gift for the other parent's birthday, the way most good families do. I never questioned this at the time, but it was clearly because celebrating a birthday was much too selfish and, I guess, secular to be worthy of time and money.

Plus, our celebration of Christmas was almost entirely religious. The biggest thing at Christmas was giving to the Lottie Moon Offering for Foreign Missions. Charlotte "Lottie" Moon was a Southern Baptist Missionary to China many years ago. The story is that she denied herself food in order to be able to provide food for the children to whom she was ministering. She went too far in this self-denial so that she died aboard ship on her way back to the USA for furlough. Every year at Christmas time the big deal in our house was how much we would each increase our gift to the Lottie Moon offering, and we had to make sure that this was by far a bigger gift than all the other gifts combined. We were essentially taught that we should feel ashamed to want or enjoy gifts for ourselves. Everything should be done for the glorification of God.

Although sports were not thought of as sin the way dancing was, it was certainly not encouraged. I taught myself to play tennis and actually became fairly good, but there was not a chance that I could have considered going out for the team. That might interfere with church activities, heaven forbid!

The nearest thing to an approved sport was a skill taught in Baptist Training Union, a Sunday evening meeting before the evening church service, called a "sword drill." Young people would stand at attention in a row with their Bibles in their right hands at their sides while the sword drill leader called out, "Attention. Draw swords. First Corinthians 13:1 (for example). Charge!" At this point we were to look up the Bible passage as fast as we could, to show how familiar we were with the Bible, and the first one to find the passage would step forward and be recognized to read the verse.

I got really good at sword drills and won a lot of contests. It was only much later as an adult that it dawned on me how militaristic this "sword drill" was.

All during my junior high and high school years I was known for my religious devotion. I stood out because I couldn't attend the school dances because the Baptist church frowned on that activity. In fact, I barely missed being elected president of the student body in junior high after getting by far the most votes on the first ballot because the rumor began being spread that if I were the student body president, there would be no more school dances. I was, however, elected class president just about every year and was frequently asked to address the student assembly or to sing a solo for some special school occasion.

When I went to high school, I became friends with a group of guys who had become active in an organization called Youth For Christ which met on Saturday nights and which had an active recruiter who hung around the high school. I had not attended any of these meetings, but this group of guys, who were all leaders in the school, recruited me because of my reputation as a strong church member who was headed for the Christian ministry. I didn't much like the Youth For Christ organization or its evangelistic emphasis, but I liked belonging to this group of school leaders. One Saturday night after a Youth For Christ rally, we decided to hold our own prayer service before we went home. We drove to a city park and were sitting in the car praying when a police car pulled up. It was the longest time before we could convince the officers that we weren't up to any hanky-panky but were instead holding a prayer service!

It was during this spontaneous prayer meeting that our little group of school leaders decided that we needed to each pick out a fellow school mate to "witness" to about the need to "accept Jesus and be saved." We encouraged each other to choose the most difficult person we could think of so that the challenge would be great. I impulsively decided to choose the fullback on the school football team who was in one of my classes. This was the biggest, "baddest" player on the team, a man who later went on to play professional football and whose nickname was "Bruiser". It was in an upstairs classroom when I decided to make my move, and I wasn't at all sure that "Bruiser" wouldn't pick me up and throw me out the window. He didn't, but my witnessing didn't work worth a damn! He snorted at me and told me to mind my own GD business. I heard later that as a pro football player he became a member of the Fellowship of Christian Athletes, and I often wondered if my ill-considered attempt to "witness" to him in high school played a part in that. If so, apologies are in order, although the "Bruiser" I knew in high school could have stood some infusing with the milk of human kindness, if that was indeed a consequence of his conversion experience.

I was still in high school when a visiting minister came to our church to hold what was called a "revival meeting". "Revivals" were a regular occurrence in Baptist churches and usually lasted an entire week, with services each morning and night. But this particular "revival" was momentous for me because it introduced me to the most magnetic personality I have ever met. The visiting minister's name was the Rev. John DeFoore. At the time of this writing, the Rev. DeFoore lives in Texas and is still active in Baptist circles. I need to describe the impact this minister's personality had on me because it helps explain why I stayed in the ministry as long as I did.

John DeFoore was a big man with a big smile and a big personality who had a way of making you feel, when you were in conversation with him, that you were the most important person in the world. In fact many a person who sat through one of his sermons would report that it felt as if DeFoore were talking only to him/her. It was an incredible gift. He was not a hell-fire and damnation preacher. Quite the contrary, he was what I would consider very liberal in his theology. However, he still preached, and obviously believed, that Jesus was sent to earth by God to bring redemption to the human race. He just did it in a unique style that made his message, and the man himself, incredibly compelling.

He claimed to be impressed with me and with my gifts for the ministry, and we began a correspondence. Before long the Rev. DeFoore had become a missionary to Alaska under the auspices of the Southern Baptist Home Mission Board. Alaska was not yet a state in those days. He was minister of a little mission church, which later became quite large, in Anchorage, AK. During my senior year in high school, I got a request from DeFoore to come to Anchorage for the summer and help him in his church, doing what was referred to as "student summer mission work." I was too young (only 18) to be appointed for this work by the Southern Baptist Home Mission Board, so we had to make other financial arrangements. The Men's Prayer Breakfast of my father's church decided to take on this project and raised money for my trip.

One hour after the end of my high school graduation ceremony I was on my way to Alaska to be a summer missionary in the Calvary Baptist Church of Anchorage.

Although I had been given money by the Men's Prayer Breakfast group, I was left to make my own travel arrangements. At 18, I hardly knew how to do that. Apparently it never occurred to anyone to question whether I had enough money to actually make the trip or to help make travel arrangements. I can only assume that everyone involved trusted that God would provide for me.

I ended up hitchhiking a ride with a man who was driving to Canada and going as far as Minot, ND, in his car, helping with the driving. From there I caught a train across to Seattle, where I realized I didn't have enough money to buy a plane ticket to Anchorage. I wired my father about my dilemma and then walked around downtown Seattle to wait for more money to arrive by telegram.

While strolling around the sidewalks of the first city outside the Bible belt I had ever been in, I chanced upon a striptease show in an old movie theater, and my hormones got the best of me. I went in. I had never seen anything so erotic, and I felt a strange mixture of delirium and despair as I left the theater – delirium because I couldn't believe there were actually women who would flaunt and celebrate their sexuality, and despair because my enjoyment of the show went against everything I had been taught! It was a minor existential crisis for this little preacher boy from Mississippi, and I resolved to never backslide (the term the church uses for carnal transgressions) again.

When I arrived in Anchorage, I told John Defoore how I had tried to witness about Christ to some strangers on the train trip to Seattle.

I most assuredly did NOT tell him about going to see the strip show!

When the summer was over and I returned stateside to enroll as a ministerial student at Mississippi College, I found myself trying to act and sound like my idol, the Rev. DeFoore, whose conversational style was unbelievably attractive. Happily, this phase of my life didn't last long, and I was soon content to just be known as one of the up-and-coming young ministers on campus. Within a few months I had a student pastorate in a rural church to which I drove every weekend, as well as spending summers either preaching or leading singing in what were called "youth revivals" in churches around the area, all of which enabled me to pay for my college education.

During my junior year in college, I received another invitation to return to Alaska to do mission work. The Rev. DeFoore was heading stateside to do some post-graduate study at the seminary and needed someone to fill his pulpit during his absence. Plus, another missionary I had met on my earlier Alaska mission needed someone to help him finish building a log church in one remote Eskimo village, Kobuk, and build another church building, with missionary residence included, in another remote Eskimo village, Selawik. When I say remote, I mean really, really remote. No roads either leading to the villages or inside them. Both villages were just squatting along the banks of the rivers for which they were named. To reach them, you had to fly in by bush plane equipped with pontoons instead of wheels and land on the river.

I interrupted my college studies, resigned my student pastorate and returned to Alaska for the better part of a year to first be the interim pastor in DeFoore's church in Anchorage and then to travel to inside the Arctic Circle to help Southern Baptist Home Missionary Dick Miller build church buildings in these remote Eskimo villages. It was hard, physical labor because there was no electricity in the villages. Everything had to be done by hand, including hand-ripping some 2 X 8's when we needed 2 X 4's. This arduous task took approximately two days with first one of us using the rip saw, then the other. When we began, we each took a 15-minute stint at ripping. By the time we finished, we could each only last about a minute before taking a breather.

Neither Dick Miller nor I knew anything about construction, but that didn't seem to matter. I was serving God and loving it!

To give you some idea of how sincere I was in my devotion to the faith, I'm including the following excerpt from a prayer I wrote out during this missionary sojourn. I copied this off of a yellowed, frayed paper on which this handwritten prayer is dated May 3, 1955.

Dear God, I recognize my dire need of Thee. Hear my humble cry and let Thy ever-comforting goodness steal over my troubled and restless mind. Let Thy healing balm sooth and cool my fevered spirit. And give me rest.

My life is filled throughout with iniquity, and I am unclean. . . . . I would be free to be pure, to be no longer repulsed by the sight of my own image, by the knowledge of my inner self. For, Oh Thou Purest of the Pure, my thoughts are ever and always carnal. I would think high and noble thoughts, but my mind and my eye plot against me. They betray me against myself.

. . . . Give answer, Oh God of my salvation, to my seeking heart. Deliver me from the sin that is me. In Jesus' name. Amen.

This prayer goes on for six pages and reveals the angst of a young minister trying to make sense of the faith he has always believed. In case you haven't figured it out, the momentous sin for which I felt so guilt-stricken was what the religious community referred to as "self-abuse". I had been taught that this was something that a true follower of Jesus would not do. So I made resolve after resolve never to indulge in this activity again, but I always failed. I was twenty years old, for crying out loud, with normal, perhaps above normal, teenage libido! And here I was trying to serve Jesus in the Alaskan wilderness and live up to an impossible, and ridiculous, religious standard. The proscription against masturbation had nothing whatever to do with genuine morality, but I didn't know that at the time. I just felt horribly guilty.

When I returned to college, I became minister in another rural church to which I drove on weekends, while I finished my BA with a major in English and minors in History and Bible. I had also already begun to have doubts about the faith. I shared my doubts with some of my ministerial student friends, many of whom agreed that these were legitimate questions, but none of whom had any answers. I tried to get help from more seasoned ministers -- my religion professors, the minister of the campus church, my father and his minister friends, and the Rev. DeFoore. All of them treated my doubts as if they were no big deal. Many reported how they, too, had entertained doubts along the way, but that God had taken the doubts away. I remember one answer which encapsulates the kind of answers I got from all the religious leaders I consulted. It was, "John, go ahead and kick the rock. You won't break it. And when you're done kicking, you'll know it is truly the Rock of Ages."

What that answer really said was, **we don't know any good answers to the questions you raise, but we found a way to stick it out, and you should, too.**

I married my college sweetheart, who had her heart set on becoming a minister's wife, worked as the interim PR director at the college after my graduation while my wife finished her degree, and we then headed off to seminary.

The seminary I chose was Southeastern Baptist Theological Seminary in Wake Forest, NC. This was the newest of the Southern Baptist seminaries and had the reputation at the time of being the most liberal. I know it may be hard to imagine the terms "liberal" and "Southern Baptist" in the same sentence, but that was before the takeover of the Southern Baptist Convention by fundamentalists. That transition occurred after I had completed my seminary training and was a part of the growth of the religious right throughout the country.

Southeastern Seminary was located on the old Wake Forest College campus in Wake Forest, NC, established in 1951 after the college was given a huge grant by the Reynolds Foundation to build a new campus in Winston-Salem, NC. I made the journey to North Carolina from Mississippi with a total of 200 borrowed dollars, a pregnant wife, and a 28-foot house trailer, determined somehow to muddle through.

The $200 soon ran out, and after going two days with no food in the house, I asked an older seminary friend who had some money tucked away from an earlier career in insurance to lend me five dollars because there wasn't even any oatmeal in the house, and my pregnant wife had to eat even if I could manage to fast. This friend insisted on lending me $15, even though I protested that I didn't know how I'd be able to repay him. He also put me in touch with a widow, who had been a former seminary student, who lent us $500 to pay for the birth of our first child. We used our house trailer for collateral and paid off both debts when we sold the trailer during my second year in seminary. They charged me no interest, and we named our first daughter after the woman whose loan paid for her delivery. There was no such thing as health insurance in those days.

We had journeyed to North Carolina with the faith that somehow God would provide so that I could get a seminary education. We began attending the campus church immediately and somehow made an impression on the church leadership. As a consequence I was soon offered the position of Youth Minister in this church (a position with lots of prestige but only a $125 a month salary), my wife got an office job in Raleigh, our first daughter was born, and we became involved in the local community. This included getting to know my seminary professors really well because most of them belonged to the campus church, and I had many of their children in the church youth programs. I sang in the church choir, often singing solos, conducted a youth choir, and was soon filling the pulpit of this church whenever the minister was away. This was a challenge for me because I found myself preaching before my seminary professors, as well as many of my fellow students.

But it also gave me easy access to talk with my professors about my theological doubts. None of them was surprised by the questions I raised because essentially all of them admitted to having, or having had, some of the same concerns. But frankly, none of them was very helpful either. Some of them suggested authors for me to read, which I dutifully did, but none of this study provided a satisfactory answer for my basic questions about the validity of the Christian faith.

I went to the senior minister of the campus church where I worked and told him of my doubts. I asked him to please not ask me to fill in for him in the pulpit for awhile, because if I did, I would only be able to talk about my uncertainties. He was very understanding. He was also incredibly bright. In fact, I rather imagine that he really didn't believe much of traditional theology either, but he was much too far along in his career to even think of making a change at that point. Besides, this particular Baptist church had a strong liberal tradition, relating to the very liberal Wake Forest University which had long since outgrown its Baptist beginnings, and whose church members, in general, were at the other extreme from fundamentalist beliefs like the virgin birth or the plenary verbal theory of the inspiration of the Bible. I suspect that few, if any, of them believed in the idea of eternal punishment, though I don't know that for certain.

Although this church didn't have "revivals" as more traditional Baptist churches did, we did have a week-long series of services led by a famous liberal minister, the Rev. Dr. George Buttrick, who was Chaplain at Harvard University at the time. I was mesmerized by Dr. Buttrick. He was by far the most learned and brilliant minister I had ever met. I didn't presume on his time by trying to talk with him about my theological doubts since he was only there for a week. But the fact that I was able to associate with him helped me decide that I should stay in the ministry. I figured that if someone as brilliant as Dr. Buttrick could be a believer, there must be something wrong with me if I couldn't. Besides, John DeFoore, my idol from teenage years, had also stayed in the ministry. So

I resolved to try to put my doubts about the faith aside, stay in the church, stay in the ministry, become as genuine a caregiver as I could be, and trust that my doubts would eventually go away.

They didn't!

My decision to stay in the ministry was also accompanied by a naive determination to be "Simon pure" in my approach to this vocation. I resolved that I was not going to play the game that I had seen played all my life by most of the ministers I knew. I'm referring to the fact that they claimed to want only to do God's will, but in reality they worked behind the scenes to become ministers of the larger, more prestigious churches. In the Southern Baptist tradition, there is no governing hierarchy to decide where ministers serve. Each church is autonomous and decides for itself whom to employ as minister. Supposedly the church prays for God's guidance, and the ministers being considered also pray to try to discover God's will.

A standard joke among my ministerial student friends, however, was that when a large, wealthy and prestigious church issued an invitation to a minister, the minister would be downstairs praying to discern God's will while his wife was upstairs packing!

I found this whole process fraudulent, disgusting and unworthy of someone who had supposedly devoted his life to trying to usher in the "Kingdom of God". I refused to participate.

When I finished seminary, I did not ask any of the many contacts I had to help me land a choice church. Since I had been relatively well-known on campus because of my position in the campus church, it was assumed that I would have several options when I graduated. I had none. Somehow God didn't seem to be paying attention. I packed up my family and moved back to Mississippi to await the Lord's directions. I refused to let my minister father use any of his contacts to help me out. After three months, quite without any input from me, I received an invitation from a small rural church in Wilkes County, North Carolina, to come preach a trial sermon. Within a month we had moved into the parsonage provided by this church and settled in to become a part of this community of hard-working, good-hearted people, mostly farmers and factory workers with no higher education. Many of them did not suffer from lack of intelligence, however, and I learned a valuable lesson, namely that education and intelligence were not always highly correlated.

Most of the ministers of the other rural churches in the county were uneducated, and I was viewed with more than a little suspicion. It was quite a switch to go from preaching to my fellow seminarians and professors to preaching in this rural church, but I had experience with this from my days as a student minister in rural churches while in college. In spite of the fact that I didn't preach the usual evangelistic message, the church prospered. It was the center of the community, and we were made to feel quite special. I worked hard at being content with simply trying to live a life of service, performing weddings, funerals, visiting the sick and sharing the life concerns of the members of this community.

We did, in fact, become accepted by the community. My wife began to refer to herself jokingly as "Em". The reason was that we were asked to dine in the homes of our parishioners on a regular basis, and the colloquial phrase that one wife said to another, sort of proudly, was "I'm having the preacher and 'em over for dinner this Sunday."

So my wife said she was "Em."

During this pastorate our second daughter was born. My wife hemorrhaged following the delivery, necessitating an emergency hysterectomy. She had lost a lot of blood, and it wasn't at all clear that she would survive. During a very long night at the hospital while she was in surgery, I wandered into the little hospital chapel in the wee hours of the morning. Overcome with emotion I found myself prostrate on the floor, agonizing that perhaps it was because of my religious doubts that all this was happening. I know this reaction doesn't make any rational sense, but that is what a lifetime of immersion in religion-induced guilt will do to you. I promised God that if He would only let my wife live so we could raise our children together, I would never doubt again.

It was not a promise I could keep no matter how hard I tried, and believe me, I DID try!

My wife recovered, our little daughter was healthy and delightful, but I was still filled with inner struggle. I felt like a fraud. I had the devil's own time (interesting play on words!) trying to find sermon material which I could preach with any degree of integrity.

I decided to enroll in the Pastoral Care program at the Baptist Hospital in Winston-Salem, about an hour's drive away. For a year I commuted every day during the week to this program of study which trained ministers to be Pastoral Counselors while still holding my pastorate in the Wilkes County church where I preached on Sundays. There was essentially zero emphasis on theology in this Pastoral Care program, and I felt much more comfortable doing this than trying to come up with sermon material that I could deliver without feeling like a fraud. When I graduated from this program of study as a certified pastoral counselor, I began to think of going back to seminary and getting a doctorate in Pastoral Psychology because I didn't think I could stay in the pastoral ministry.

I approached my father, who was a long-time Rotarian, about whether his Rotary Club in Mississippi would consider sponsoring me for a Rotary scholarship so that I could afford to go back to seminary for a doctoral program in Pastoral Psychology. However, this was during the height of the civil rights movement, and the murder of the three young civil rights volunteers in Philadelphia, Mississippi, had recently occurred. Philadelphia was only a few miles from where my parents lived. I had written an article that was published in the North Carolina Baptist newspaper, the Biblical Recorder, in which I wrote that I was ashamed of Mississippi, the state of my birth, because of these atrocities. The article began, "There is a cold rain falling outside. It is also raining inside of me. I just learned about the murders in my home state of Mississippi. And I am ashamed." When I asked my dad about the possibility of a Rotary scholarship sponsorship, he made it clear that members of his local club had received a copy of my article and were not at all pleased with the public stance I had taken. No scholarship money for the likes of me!

Then came an invitation to become the minister of a larger church in Winston-Salem, and I decided that maybe that would be the answer to my discontent. We adopted our third child, a son, and moved to the city. But I hadn't been in this pastorate more than six months when I knew that this move had not been the answer. I remember specifically that when I would be mowing the lawn, a mindless activity, my mind would race with thoughts of desperation at my predicament. What could I possibly do? My congregation was happy with me, but I wasn't happy with myself! The church was growing, and I was something of a local celebrity, but I was dying inside!

I was determined not to end up like so many ministers I had come to know: publicly phony and privately cynical!

The average parishioner would be thunderstruck to know how many ministers don't actually believe half of what they preach. This is especially true if the minister has received a good theological education, not just what is essentially a "Bible School" education which most fundamentalist seminaries offer. The more you learn about what kind of book the Bible is, how standard theology came to be accepted, about the incredibly embarrassing history of religion through the ages, the more you have to see that the whole thing just doesn't hold water. That is, if you are willing to take an honest look at the evidence.

I read voraciously. One of the books I read was The Christian Agnostic by Leslie Weatherhead, a British minister who tried to address thorny theological questions with integrity. He defined a Christian agnostic as one who was strongly influenced by the story of Jesus (which could also be called the Christ myth), but who affirmed only those articles of the faith which had validated themselves in his own experience. Everything else was to be put in a mental drawer labeled "awaiting further light." This provided temporary comfort, but it was not enough.

My mental drawer was getting filled to the brim!

I knew I didn't believe any of the major tenets of the Christian faith. I had read the Bible very carefully and knew that it couldn't possibly be the Word of God. Too many horrible passages, inconsistencies, and inaccuracies! I knew I didn't believe in the virgin birth or that Jesus was God become flesh. I didn't believe in any kind of life after death, either in hell or heaven, or that Jesus had been bodily raised from the dead. I didn't believe that confessing your sins and accepting Jesus as "Savior" automatically transformed anyone. It became very clear to me that if there were a God who was in charge of what happened in the world, He must be sleeping on the job because horrendous things kept happening on both a local and worldwide scale. And I came to see that most churches didn't really spend much of their resources helping the most vulnerable among us, but rather most of their donated resources went into keeping the institution going.

I was filled with incredible angst. I hadn't wanted to hurt my parents by leaving the ministry while I was a ministerial student in college, and I still didn't want to hurt them. I could not imagine making that phone call to tell them that I was leaving the ministry. That was much more of a concern for me than how I could think of changing careers at that stage of my life and how I would support my family. I had confidence that I would be able to start another career, but I had been a minister all my life. All my friends were either ministers or very devoted church members.

However, it became increasingly clear that if I were to have any sense of genuine integrity, I had no choice but to bite the bullet and leave the ministry.

The church of which I was pastor had seen a

succession of ministers before me who had not stayed very long or who had had other problems. For that reason, even though I knew for certain within six months after accepting that pastorate that I would have to end up leaving the ministry, I didn't think it was fair to them not to stay at least three years in my position. I essentially wasted three more years just trying to struggle through each Sunday, but I was determined to try to be considerate of my parishioners even if it was tearing my guts out.

That, and the fact that I dreaded making that phone call to Mississippi. I had put it off as long as I could – not because I thought they would be angry or try to persuade me that I was making a serious mistake, but because I knew how much they would be devastated.

I was their hope of carrying on the tradition of Baptist ministers in the Compere lineage started five generations before by the original Compere missionary to this country, Lee. By leaving the ministry I was sabotaging that tradition and ending that history. All hope for continuing the Compere family tradition of ministry was now gone.

By the time I finally made that phone call, I essentially had no choice. My mental drawer was crammed full with things I was supposed to believe, but couldn't. I was being eaten alive by the feeling that I was living a lie, saying prayers which were heart-felt but intellectually dishonest, since I was convinced that no one was listening. At least, not anyone supernatural.

I rehearsed the phone call in my mind dozens of times, trying to find a way to say what had to be said. There was no good way.

With great reluctance, I made the call.

There was stunned silence on the other end. I had tried talking with my parents years earlier when I was in seminary about my serious doubts concerning the validity of the faith I had been taught, but they had assumed that this was just a phase I was going through and that I would resolve my doubts on the side of belief. My father even said that when these doubts were over, I would have an even stronger faith than before. My phone call forced him to admit that had not happened. They were, in fact, devastated. How could they explain this to their friends, all of whom were either also Baptist ministers or, at least, stalwart church members?

Years later my mother confirmed my reluctance to come clean about the fact that I no longer believed what I had been taught. She told me that she was convinced that if I had followed my strong inclinations to leave the ministry after my first year in seminary, it might have actually resulted in my father's early death.

When I think of how I wasted an unnecessary ten years of my young adult life by continuing my struggle to remain in the church, I comfort myself with the thought at least I didn't risk causing an untimely death of my father, a man who was truly sincere in his faith and his dedication to it. I don't think he would have actually died had I told him earlier, but there is no question that it would have caused him unbelievable pain.

Long after I had become a PhD clinical psychologist and no longer even tried to engage my parents in any discussions of my reasons for leaving the church, I was able to be frank about what it was like growing up in such an all-inclusive religious atmosphere.

Here is an excerpt from a letter I wrote my father when he continued to try to explain my leaving the ministry on any grounds except my genuine inability to believe Christian theology, like the notion that he and my mother must have been bad parents for this to have happened.

"If I could have had anything different, I'd have had less religious absorption, more freedom to make my own choices about how to move through the world. The family took a back seat to the church, which was and is almost the end-all and be-all with you. But, hey, it could have been a lot worse! And although I am in almost complete disagreement with you theologically, I honor your faith. I learned a lot from you both about integrity. That's how I try to live my life – warts and all."

At age 32, with three children to support, I made the decision that I would go to graduate school in psychology so that I could become a clinical psychologist.

It was a much-delayed and unbelievably difficult decision, but it was also the most liberating experience of my life. I could now let my mind take me wherever it wanted to go. Others could believe whatever they wanted to, but I would only accept what made sense to me, what I found supported by the evidence.

It truly felt like bursting free from lifelong shackles!

When I resigned my church, I didn't publicly admit that I was no longer a believer. I don't know whether this was the best thing to do or not. My intention was to cause as little upset as possible to those who had looked up to me as a spiritual leader. If their faith was working for them, I didn't want to rock the boat.

I enrolled in Wake Forest University, which was across town, taking both undergraduate and graduate psychology courses because I didn't have an academic psychology background. Because of my good academic record I was fortunate enough to receive scholarship money from the National Science Foundation to help pay for this schooling which resulted in a MA in psychology, but I also had to supplement our income by being a minister on the weekends, serving as an Auxiliary Chaplain at an Air Force Radar Station nearby and occasionally filling the pulpit when a minister was away. My wife took a job at the Dean of Women's office on campus. I also became a graduate teaching assistant and taught some undergraduate psychology courses.

Upon completing my MA, I applied to several graduate schools so I could go on for my doctorate. One of them was Harvard University, where miraculously I was accepted. I suspect that they were interested in diversity, and a former Baptist minister was not the usual applicant! I remember that the acceptance letter began "Welcome to Harvard!" with the obvious assumption that anyone who was accepted into prestigious Harvard University would certainly enroll. But that was in 1969, and the "Yippies" had just taken over Harvard Square. The thought of moving my three little children into that turmoil was more than I could contemplate. Instead, I accepted a wonderful scholarship from the University of North Carolina at Chapel Hill, which was only an hour and a half's drive away. We would continue living in Winston-Salem. My wife wouldn't have to change jobs, and my children wouldn't have to change schools. For three years I commuted to Chapel Hill from Winston-Salem to earn my Ph.D. in clinical psychology.

My motto during these grueling years was the mock Latin phrase, "Non carburundum illigitimatis est", which is, being interpreted, "don't let the bastards grind you down!"

Upon receiving my doctorate I settled down to teaching psychology at Wake Forest University and Bowman Gray School of Medicine, plus having a private clinical practice of Psychology, and finally being free from the excruciating bind of having my professional career demand a belief in supernatural things for which I found no credible evidence.

My personal life suffered from all this mid-life disruption, however. My wife and I became involved in the marriage enrichment movement guided by Dr. David Mace and his wife Vera and began leading marriage enrichment retreats. At one point we were approached about becoming the leaders of the Association of Couples for Marriage Enrichment when the Maces were nearing retirement. But we declined because all the good communication skills we were teaching had revealed that our own marriage had some serious difficulties, not the least of which was my leaving the ministry. My wife had been a cooperative partner in helping me change careers, working full-time to help pay the bills. She could not have been more supportive of my need to make this drastic change. However, who I had become in this process was not really what she had bargained for when we married.

I have often said that she was the perfect minister's wife; she just wasn't married to the perfect minister!

Sadly, three years after I received my doctorate, my marriage of 20 years came to an end. Within weeks after we separated, my wife, soon to be my ex-wife, became very active in the Baptist church again, singing in the choir and later serving as a Deacon in her very progressive church. There were other factors besides my rejection of religion that played a part in our divorce, but none of them involved any hint of scandal. We have remained good friends, worked well together in continuing to raise our three children, including my performing the marriage ceremonies for all three of them with their mother serving as wedding director. Although the divorce was painful for all of us, certainly for our children, we made it a point to never say an unkind word about the other, and our children have since said that, if divorce had to happen, we managed to handle it about as well at it could be done.

Within a few years I left academia and moved out into a full-time private practice of Clinical Psychology, became a consultant at the Center for Creative Leadership in nearby Greensboro, and through that contact began speaking professionally at conferences and conventions on "Psychology You Can Use." Eventually I closed my clinical practice and became a full-time professional speaker, my many years in the pulpit and inherited proclivity for public speaking serving me well in this forum.

On the professional speaking platform I never made any mention of the fact that I had a theological degree and was still an ordained Southern Baptist minister. (In this religious tradition, there is no protocol for remanding an ordination; I'm sure, however, if Baptist authorities had known what I actually believed and if there had been a way to do it, I would have been de-frocked summarily!) However, the emphasis in my speeches on living ethically and treating others with kindness as the best route to "life satisfaction" often led people to think that I must be a person of religious faith. (Unfortunately, many people still make the mistake of equating ethical morality with religious belief, an assumption the majority of secular humanists are hard at work to disprove.)

Most of the time when, following a platform presentation, an audience member would ask about my church affiliation, I would find a way to deflect the question, because I had not been hired by the corporate meeting planner to try to change people's religious beliefs. However, there was one particular occasion when the questioner would not be dissuaded from his quest to find out what I believed. So I admitted to being a member of the Unitarian-Universalist church, which I was at the time.

He was aghast at this answer because he apparently knew something about the UU denomination. I had a very difficult time drawing this conversation to a close. Within a few days I received the following letter from this man whose genuine concern for me was evident:

Dear Dr. Compere:

Your talk to the (name omitted) group in Scottsdale was truly inspiring, and most all of us are hopeful that you will accept (our company's) invitation to return in eighteen months to our Disney World meeting. I particularly appreciated your speaking to me afterwards regarding your thoughts about heaven and hell, God and the Bible.

You likely have little need to hear more from a religious man who espouses stuff you were taught as a child but have long since rejected. Maybe rejected is too strong, since you did say it was stored away awaiting further revelation. Far be it from me, a salesman with a mere BA in business, to consider myself a significant source of revelation to a man as learned as you. I did sense that you enjoyed our dialogue, though, so I will risk sharing a few more thoughts. If you've had enough, just stop reading now, throw away this letter, and you've heard the last of me. I will still eagerly anticipate hearing you again in Disney World, particularly since my four sons will be there, and I'd really like for them to hear you.

Dr. Compere, it seems your main reason for shelving Christianity is the apparent unfairness of God sending people who have never heard to hell. I, too, believe God to be fair and have no answer for that dilemma, at least none you haven't already heard, and none that totally resolves the matter in my mind either.

A much more significant matter, though, causes me to shelve that one question rather than to throw out Christianity altogether. The biggest question that we must answer is whether or not Jesus was God. If the answer is NO, we can throw away our Bibles, become hedonists, eat, drink, and be merry, take from the rich, keep a commission, give the rest to the poor, or keep it all if we need it, and live it up until we die.

If the answer is YES, then everything He said is absolute truth and woe to anyone who rejects His words. (Here the letter writer quotes some Bible verses.)

The following thoughts were brought to my attention by C. S. Lewis in the book MERE CHRISTIANITY. You said you have read the book so you may be familiar with these ideas. . . .Mr. Lewis was an atheist who came to an acceptance of Jesus Christ as God through logic rather than blind faith. (Not very *common.) He concluded that Jesus had to be one of three things:*

An imposter – the devil himself playing a major trick

A lunatic – like one who thinks of himself as a poached egg

God Himself – what He claimed to be.

. . . Dr. Compere, I have three questions to which I would be most honored if you would respond. Please believe me that I'm not trying to corner you, but this is all so clear to me. My faith in Christ brings such peace to my soul. It gives me assurance of eternal life. The millstone of fear of the end is removed, and the freedom to live and love knowing my wrong-doings are forgiven and I am clean before Him make everything else in life pale into insignificance. . .

So it is my desire for you to know God that prompts my writing, and even if I never hear from you, I want to say again how much I enjoyed your talk and how I hope to be able to hear from you again. . .

My questions are:

Do you agree with C. S. Lewis that Jesus had to be one of the three things mentioned?

If so, which one do you say He is, and do you agree with Lewis' conclusions regarding that choice?

If not, what additional options do you feel exist?

If you think I'm full of beans, please don't fear that I will be despondent or hurt or anything else if you tell me. I'd just really like to know how you feel about all of this.

Most sincerely,

Johnson D. Doe (real person, fictitious name)

The above letter was written in 1992. Below is a

copy of my immediate reply.

Dear Mr. Doe:

I'm set to try succinctly to respond to your thoughtful letter. I appreciate your concern for me, and it makes sense since you believe that unless I believe as you do, I am doomed. My response is not intended to sway you in the least. If your faith truly brings "peace to your soul," as I'm delighted to know it does, the last thing I would want to do is influence you regarding that in any way.

Question 1: Do I agree with Lewis that Jesus had to be either an imposter, lunatic, or God? Absolutely not. That argument makes good pulpit rhetoric, but it doesn't begin to exhaust the possibilities. I'll mention only one: this premise assumes that what we have in the Bible is accurate reporting. Many very thoughtful Biblical scholars offer very convincing evidence that this is not the case. I rather doubt that the man Jesus claimed to be God. I suspect that the phrase he is reported to have most often used, Son of Man, is a more accurate portrayal of his claims.

Question 2: Since my answer to #1 is No, this question doesn't really obtain, except for me to say again that I don't think Jesus was God (and doubt that he claimed to be), but that I think his reported story is, in the main, a wonderful example of how to live a life of integrity and kindness, honesty and self-sacrifice. He was clearly a very true window through which the light shone, though not, in my opinion, the only such window.

Question 3: What other options? Plenty. One of which is the one that fits for me, namely to live my life with as much integrity as I am capable. I have no fear of death either, although I do not know what lies on the other side, if anything. I must also add neither does anyone else know what lies beyond. If someone says, "But I do so know – I know because I have the assurance of the Word of God and because I know it in my heart!", then I have to gently say, that is one's belief speaking, not one's knowledge. The fact that someone believes that the Bible is the infallible Word of God doesn't necessarily make it so. Of course, I'm aware it doesn't make it necessarily NOT so either. Each person chooses what makes most sense to him or her.

You made the erroneous assumption that the only reason I don't accept traditional Christian theology is the problem with a just and fair God condemning people to eternal punishment. That is by no means the only reason. In fact, so that you won't worry further that I somehow have just not considered this matter carefully enough and that if I could just "know God" as you know Him, I would be converted, let me say that I have also been where you are. If I were to send you copies of the prayers I wrote out daily back in the '50's while I was a missionary in an Eskimo village in Alaska, you would hear the yearnings of as devout a heart as any current Bible-believing Christian. Likewise, when I visit my aged parents and attend a service where my father is preaching and I sing whatever special music selection he requests with all the sincerity of my being, you would find it hard to reject the authenticity of my theological stance, all the while not agreeing with it for yourself. My father loves "I Walked Today Where Jesus Walked", and I often sing that at his request when I am able to attend a service with them. I don't believe in their theology, but I believe in them, and I honor their faith.

No, it isn't that I haven't wrestled and struggled to

believe the traditional faith. It is that I cannot. The fact that C. S. Lewis converted from atheism (to believerhood) is not as unusual as you might think, although conversions from faith to reason are much more common. But it is totally irrelevant. I respect Lewis also. I just do not agree with his conclusions.

If, for whatever reason, you wish to explore this further, let me suggest a book by a Christian minister Leslie Weatherhead entitled THE CHRISTIAN AGNOSTIC. I also do not agree with all of what he writes, but he explores some dimensions of the issues which Lewis did not. (If I were writing the same response today, I'd mention many other books by authors like Hitchens, Dawkins, Harris, Barker, and Mills, which books were not around in the early '90s.)

I hope you did not really mean what you said as we talked and you reiterated in your letter that if the traditional Christian belief is somehow not accurate, you would live a distinctly different life. If you do mean that, I cannot help thinking how sad that is. Because to live life the way Jesus and other great religious teachers and philosophers have taught is clearly superior to any "Eat, drink . . ." kind of sybaritic lunacy. Surely you wouldn't seriously change your ethics if you thought there were no eternal punishment awaiting you for doing so. Why in the world would any serious follower of Jesus do that? It seems to me that such a position vitiates the heart of the faith one espouses. Surely your experience of life satisfaction from the way your faith helps you live would not lead you to choose a life of dereliction and dissipation if you thought there were no hell waiting for you for doing so. People who live like that create their own hell. Life is infinitely more meaningful, satisfying, and rewarding if lived with integrity.

Thank you again for your kind words about my presentation. I'm happy to report that I have agreed to return at the Orlando convention. So I'll look forward to seeing you again there and to meeting your sons.

Warm personal regards,

John S. Compere, Ph.D.

P.S. I'm remembering a little poem that I'd like to share with you, though I can't remember the author. And in so sharing it, I don't mean to imply that you are rejecting me – only that the traditional position does, in fact, reject other positions, no matter how thoughtful and personally authentic. And I think that is decidedly un-Christlike. So the poem goes:

He drew a circle that shut me out
Heretic, rebel, a thing to flout.
But love and I had the wit to win:
We drew a circle that took him in.

I hope I live long enough to see this country, indeed the entire world, begin to reject the nonsense that what makes a person moral is religion, and to see more and more intelligent people who value reason give themselves permission to outgrow religion, to give credence to evidence, to burst free from faith.

Towards that end, the rest of this book is dedicated.

Great Great Grandfather Lee Compere's grave is in the Hamilton-Beaman Cemetery in Retreat, Navarro County, Texas

Circa 1840: Pioneer Baptist missionary and preacher. Rev. Lee Compere and second wife Sarah Beck.

Great Grandfather William Samuel Compere married Louisa Gabilla Stephens in 1859. It was her second marriage after the death of Orleander Love. Graduated Georgetown College, Kentucky, Class of 1857, Teaching Diploma. He served as Sergeant/Chaplain, Company K, 36th Mississippi Infantry Regiment and is listed on the National Park Service records as paroled after his capture at the Battle of Vicksburg. He rejoined his unit and continued until his discharge in May, 1865.

Above Far Right Sitting: Great Grandfather William Samuel Compere graduated from Georgetown Baptist College in Kentucky and came back to teach religion at Mississippi College, Clinton, MS, also serving rural churches as minister. He served in as Chaplain in 36th Regiment, Mississippi Infantry. Captured at Vicksburg in 1863.

Above Far Left Sitting: Grandfather Ebenezer John Compere graduated from Mississippi College, became a minister then died in 1912 from falling off a ladder while helping a parishioner raise a barn. My father was five when he died.

IN MEMORIAM

" Rev. E. J. Compere, one of the members of our Church, died this the 25th. of April 1912, as a result of a fall from a barn.

Bro. Compere was one of the most consistent and valuable members of our Church. He was faithful in attendance upon all of our services, - teaching a class in Sunday School regularly and being present at nearly all of our Prayer Meetings. He was liberal in his giving, always giving all he could to advance our Lord's Kingdom. Our Church will greatly miss him. He will not only be missed in our Church but in our town as well. He was a good and honest citizen, a loving, kind, and faithful husband, a gentle and patient father, (a painstaking teacher), an earnest and true preacher, a careful and punctual carpenter and an earnest and thorough teacher.

He has gone from us, but though he is dead his works do follow him.

He leaves a wife and four children with whom we deeply sympathize and for whom we shall pray God's Choicest blessings."

Signed: Rev. Zeno Wall, his Pastor
Mt. Olive Baptist Church
Mt. Olive, Mississippi

Above: Memorium letter on the death of my grandfather, Ebenezer John Compere.

Circa 1950s: My parents, the Rev. William Lowrey Compere and Jacqueline Senter Compere. William Carey University has the Clarke/Compere Endowed Scholarship established in 2002 in memory of Lowrey and Jacqueline Compere. This scholarship provides financial assistance for a male student preparing for a career in the ministry or a female student pursuing a career in speech education.

Northside Baptist Church
"THE CHURCH WITH A CHALLENGE"

W. LOWREY COMPERE, Pastor
SYLVIA BURR, Educational Secretary

Sunday, April 6, 1952

APRIL
1945

APRIL
1952

Rev. John Compere

Grace Baptist Revival Starts Monday

PASTOR'S SEVENTH ANNIVERSARY

Today is the seventh anniversary of the coming of our Pastor to Northside. During these seven years under his leadership, God has greatly blessed our church, and we take this opportunity to express to Brother Compere our sincere love and appreciation for what he has meant to us. So many would like today to express individual gratitude for the hours he has spent in wise counsel in personal problems; others are remembering his unfailing comfort in hours of sorrow; and all of us have felt the uplift of his Christ-like character. As pulpiteer, teacher, and visitor our Pastor is our constant inspiration.

Our members as one person will want to join in prayer that the Lord's richest blessings will be upon our Pastor and his family as they enter the eighth year of service for the Master at Northside. We have learned to love each of them and hope there will be many more years of fellowship together in the work of our Lord.

Grace Baptist Church will have its fall Revival October 5-11. The visiting speaker will be Rev. John Compere, pastor of Oaklawn Baptist Church in Winston-Salem. The services will begin each evening at 7:30 p. m. There will be special music each night. The nursery will be open for all services. Everyone is cordially invited to attend. Rev. Calvin W. Freeman is the pastor.

Above Left: William Lowrey Compere – Graduated from Mississippi College, served as minister in churches in Mississippi and Louisiana, then became President of a small Baptist Junior College in Newton, MS, where he remained until he retired at 72. He died at age 92.

Above Right and Right: John Senter Compere – Graduated from Mississippi College in 1956 and from Southeastern Baptist Theological Seminary in 1961. He withdrew from the ministry in 1967 and received an MA in Psychology from Wake Forest University in 1969 and a PhD in Clinical Psychology from the University of North Carolina, Chapel Hill in 1972.

Above: This is when I was a full-time professional speaker and was presenting a talk on "Psychology You Can USE" to an audience of 8000 at a convention in San Francisco.

Left: This is a shot of me as a Clinical Psychologist in a therapy session. This photo appeared in a psychology text-book.

THE SAD HISTORY OF THE CHURCH

When most Christians think of the church, they think of their own particular congregation, which in many cases is like an extended family. This local church has a familiar tradition, an established place in the community, and its own history which, with some occasional bumps, is generally mostly positive to its members. Many, perhaps most, of these local church members cannot imagine life without their church. It is a part of who they are, one of their main self-identifications when they meet new people.

So for this chapter to refer to the "sad" history of the church may be more than a little jarring.

I really understand this reaction, and I will be the first to admit that the local church has, across the years, earned an influential place in the lives of its members. I have no illusions that such local churches are going to lose their unique influence anytime soon. Perhaps never.

In this chapter I will unabashedly acknowledge some of the very positive contributions the church has made to our world, and I will make a plaintive plea that the modern church find a way to keep its positive aspects, while distancing itself from the unsupportable theological claims which underlie its existence, a plea that will be as radical as it is unlikely to be implemented.

But before considering the many positive things to be said about local church congregations, honesty demands that we take a candid look at the overall story of what believers consider to be the earthly "body of Christ." That story is anything but pretty, or even benign. The idea that the history of this institution is what the God of the universe intended when He, as the Bible puts it, "became flesh and dwelt among us" is utterly and absolutely indefensible.

Let me repeat that in another way so that you can't miss it. If the church is a human institution, its history is still horrible, but it is understandable because all human institutions have their share of rottenness within them. If on the other hand the church is the creation of the God of the universe, there is no way under the sun to understand the sad history of the church.

Let's take an unflinching look at that history.

To begin with, we have only the vaguest idea of what early churches were like in the first centuries after Jesus' reported crucifixion and resurrection, before the Christian religion was formally made the state religion of the Roman Empire by Constantine early in the fourth century. What we do know from the various writings which have been handed down from those days, some of them included in the Bible, some of them not, is that there was anything but unanimity among the believers. Rather, there was fierce disagreement about almost anything you can imagine, from important matters like whether Jesus was really divine or simply a wondrous human prophet, to ridiculous matters like whether women should be allowed to hold positions of authority in the group or whether men believers had to submit to cutting off the foreskins of their penises in order to be accepted into the fellowship of believers.

Let me interrupt this discussion of church history for a moment to ask you to consider, logically and with an open mind, the whole issue of circumcision and its importance in Judeo-Christian history. What circumcision refers to, of course, is the removal of the foreskin at the end of the male penis. A few centimeters of skin which grows naturally in all males. The Christian religion would have otherwise intelligent people believe that the eternal "I AM", the all-knowing, all-powerful ruler of the universe gives a flying fig about whether males submit to having that little bit of skin on the end of their penises removed or decide to leave it in place. In point of fact, most circumcised males didn't have a choice, since the procedure was (and still is) generally performed while the child is a helpless infant. But the point is, can you really imagine that if there really were someone in charge of what happens in the world, with all of its challenges, horrors, and promise, this almighty being would be focused on less than an ounce of skin on the penises of his male followers. Come on, now, be honest. Can you really imagine that? If you can, you are much more credulous than I am, Charlie Brown!

Of course, Christians will claim that this procedure is no longer required since Jesus came to fulfill divine prophecy, which is what the argument about circumcision in the early church was about, but

Christians would still have to admit that this same God who supposedly sent Jesus to redeem mankind had originally demanded that His chosen people submit to this pointless ritual. At least the male members of God's special people which, let's face it, are the only really important people in any of the Abrahamic religions of Judaism, Christianity, and Islam.

Or at least they were until early creators of the Jesus story decided that he should have been born of a virgin, as were the other heroic savior gods of the day, and they came up with the story of Mary's pregnancy by the Holy Spirit. This resulted in a significant idolization of Mary in certain church traditions, although it still didn't really make women the equal of men in any practical way in the church. Men still held all the power, with women expected to follow along docilely.

In any event, there were apparently all sorts of ridiculous arguments going on in the early church congregations during the first three centuries after the Jesus story got its start. Many of the letters of Paul which comprise the majority of the New Testament were written to deal with settling the disagreements which characterized the early church. This went on for three hundred years, folks, longer than the United States has been a country! It was a time of superstition, rumor, and a very limited world view which allowed all sorts of religious beliefs to take hold. One of these was the one which we now know as Christianity, but the main mission of these early believers seemed to be to get other people to agree with them, not to try to transform society or genuinely usher in the "kingdom of God" with peace on earth among men of good will. All indications are that the early church was much more interested in being right than in doing good.

I hate to tell you, but that is the attitude which has been most characteristic of the church throughout history down to this very day!

Roman Catholics like to imagine that the apostle Simon Peter was the first Pope because of the statement from Jesus recorded in Matthew that changed Peter's name from Simon to Peter (meaning "the rock") and said that on this "rock" would Jesus build His church and that the gates of hell would not prevail against it. We really have very little idea, though lots of conjecture, about what happened between this supposed declaration at Caesarea Philippi by Simon Peter that Jesus was the Christ (Messiah) and what emerged many centuries later as the Christian church, a politically powerful entity with tentacles throughout most of the civilized world of the West. What we do know simply confirms the idea that through the first four or five hundred years following the Jesus story the organization of believers was more concerned with power and orthodoxy than with anything Jesus may have taught about doing unto others as you would have them do unto you.

In other words, the early church focused on "I'm right and you're wrong, and if I get enough power, I'll crush you." Not exactly an inspiring example!

Of course, this was the Bronze Age when most of what we know today about how the world works was a mystery. This was a time characterized by belief in dark, demonic forces which existed for the purpose of making the lives of human beings miserable and of the almost universal belief in God (or gods) as forces which, if he (they) so chose, could intervene on behalf of humans against the powers of evil.

Has it ever occurred to you to wonder just why the idea of the devil, or demons, came about? Why should some evil being exist whose primary purpose would be to wreak havoc on the lives of struggling human beings and take pleasure in doing so? The answer is very simple: all life is fraught with danger, pain, and disease, and all life eventually ends in death. Rather than acknowledge this simple and inescapable reality, Bronze Age humans continued the myths of earlier human societies, which were ignorant of the way the world works compared to today's scientific understanding, that these misfortunes wouldn't happen if it weren't for malevolent forces which fought against the godly forces.

So, in any event, the early church was completely unable to raise itself above the Bronze Age beliefs which characterized that time in human history. Actually, I'm not being critical of the early church for being a product of its time. It makes sense that it would be IF -- and this is a most important IF -- the church is a completely human institution, not a divine one. If the church were really a product of God's intervention in human affairs, established by God (in the person of Jesus) for the purpose of doing God's will and revealing God's plan for humankind, wouldn't you think that it would have been able to rise above the human ignorance of its day to at least some degree, however small?

Well, it didn't. The Christian church was, and is, the most human of institutions, with all the failures and foibles of every other human institution. This wouldn't have been so bad if the church hadn't claimed to be of divine origin and if it hadn't become so unbelievably powerful.

But become powerful it did, and because unchecked power almost inevitably leads to corruption, the Christian church ushered in a millennium-long era of what is now often referred to as "the Dark Ages". Make no mistake -- the church was not just a part of the Dark Ages; the church was the primary **cause** of the Dark Ages!

The term Dark Ages was first used by the Italian poet Petrarch in the 14th Century CE. It describes the roughly 1000 years from the time of Constantine until the beginning of the Italian Renaissance, the years when the Christian church was more powerful than any of the governments in the countries of Europe.

There are many reasons that the description of this thousand years as "dark" is appropriate, almost all of them having to do with the fact that the Christian church was the most powerful institution in the countries of the former Roman Empire. Let's look at a few of them.

Since Christians had been persecuted at least some of the time in the first three centuries after the Jesus story, wouldn't you think that once their faith became the official religion of the day, they would want to be kind and understanding of those who held to different beliefs? If Christianity really were a religion of peace and of doing unto others as you would have them do unto you, that would have been how the church should have reacted, right?

Well, I can promise you, that is not what happened. Instead, the church became vicious in its attempt to wipe out all remnants of other religions. Christians immediately began destroying all of what they called "pagan" temples, never mind that many of them were works of architectural beauty. And the priests and priestesses of these temples were routinely imprisoned, tortured, and killed. The manner of these executions is more gruesome than you can imagine, including stoning, burning alive, beheading, dismembering. And for what? For holding to a belief different from that of the Christian church!

One horrible example is of Hypatia of Alexandria, a philosopher/mathematician of the fourth century who is credited with several creative breakthroughs in science, including the invention of the hydrometer to measure the thickness of liquids. Hypatia was reportedly very beautiful, as well as accomplished, and her counsel was sought by many learned men, something most unusual for a woman in that time. On her way home from a lecture her chariot was waylaid by a mob of Christians who stripped her naked, ripped the flesh off her body with broken pottery, dragged her through the streets of Alexandria and set her afire at the church. This is just one of thousands of such stories of savagery in the name of the Christian faith.

There were many libraries throughout the Hellenistic world, which contained countless priceless volumes from the intelligentsia of the ancient world. Well, it would never do for people to be able to read those scrolls, so they were routinely burned, the librarians executed, and the buildings which housed these literary works destroyed. This practice continued throughout the entire time of the Dark Ages. The obvious purpose was to stifle any scientific inquiry and to keep the populace ignorant of everything except what the Christian church taught. In fact, "Saint" Augustine is reported to have said that since God has spoken to us, it is no longer necessary for us to think!

Not only did the Christian church persecute and kill people who held to a different religion, or to no religion, but they also would not allow anyone within their own faith to disagree with any doctrine which the church had decreed was orthodox. As the church hierarchy grew more powerful, more and more time was spent on ferreting out beliefs within the faithful which were considered heretical. Anyone who dared to question an official position of the church was in for big trouble. Early on in the history of the church, these disagreements about matters of faith were handled with excommunication, telling the "heretical" believers that they were no longer welcome within the fellowship of believers. This happened more times than can be counted and resulted in vicious schisms within the church, many of which continue today.

However, as the church become even more powerful, its leaders were not satisfied to simply cut off a disagreeing Christian from the rest of the group, and the church began using imprisonment, torture, and execution, no matter how piously and sincerely the disagreement was defended. This resulted in horrible movements like the Inquisition in which people were accused of heresy, allowed to confess to the heresy and repent, or convicted of the heresy, tortured and killed. Sometimes if the helpless people who were charged with heresy confessed and repented, they were strangled before being burned, whereas if they refused to confess, they were burned alive. Many of the atrocities of the Inquisition also targeted Jews whose crime was only that they had not abandoned their own faith for Christianity, never mind that they supposedly worshipped the same God of Abraham as did the Christians. The Inquisitions lasted until relatively modern times, with the last of them being held in 18th Century Portugal.

Some of the most egregious atrocities of the Inquisition involved the obsession with witchcraft. Throughout the history of the Christian church there was the almost universal belief that witches actually exist. These supposed witches were usually women. In fact, it was an asserted that women were more carnal than men and thus more susceptible to being influenced by the devil into becoming witches. Some of the accusations against those who were suspected of being witches would be almost humorous if the reality of these mock trials were not so horrendous in consequence. For instance, witches were reported to have stolen men's penises, though there is no mention of what they did with them! Want to know my guess about how that accusation arose? I'll bet dollars to donuts that it came from the fact of erectile dysfunction, which surely existed in that day as well as now. When men were no longer able to perform sexual intercourse because of lack of penile erection, they had to find someone to blame. So of course, they blamed women! Thus, the myth of a witch being able to steal a man's penis was born. Or at least that is my best guess.

Of course, one of the best-known realities of intolerance by the church is the history of the Crusades, which were considered "holy wars" against the Muslin "infidels" who inhabited what Christians considered the Holy Land. Beginning in the 11th Century CE, there were a total of seven such "holy wars" in which faithful Christians were encouraged to join in organized efforts to remove all Muslims from places considered holy to Christianity. The word "crusade" comes from the Latin word for "cross". All members of the crusading armies were given cloth crosses to sew on the shoulders of their uniforms. The atrocities committed during these religious wars were almost unbelievable, except that any study of the history of the Abrahamic religions (Judaism, Christianity, and Islam) is so rife with such atrocities that students almost become inured to the outrage. These efforts of the crusaders did not ultimately succeed, but they did pave the way for the intense hostility which has characterized relationships between Christianity and Islam down to the present time.

Many Protestants claim that these atrocities were committed NOT by the true church of Jesus Christ, but by the Roman Catholic "perversion" of Christianity, while the genuine Christians went along because they had no choice and no power. The Southern Baptist tradition in which I grew up maintained that all during this time of corruption by the established church, namely the two main branches of Catholicism -- Roman and Eastern Orthodox -- there was a smattering of "real" Christians who were much like Baptists, who followed the true teachings of Jesus without being corrupted by power. It's a plaintive argument, unfortunately not supported by any credible historical evidence, which may have some minuscule validity. Namely, there were very likely many common believers who were genuinely kind, accepting, forgiving, willing to help the unfortunate among them, just as there are today in many churches, both Protestant and Catholic, no matter how exclusive the pulpit-proclaimed theology may be. But, as I discuss in the chapter on being born again, this is very likely NOT because of their particular faith and/or conversion experience, but rather because that's the kind of people they are and would have been, with or without a conversion experience or a church affiliation.

I think of the many wonderful people I have known in the church, virtually all of whom would probably claim that any goodness they exhibited came from their faith, which I'm absolutely convinced is not so. My mother is a good example. If there were such a thing as being a saint, she would have qualified in spades. There was not a mean bone in her body. Her mother before her was the same way. It was a genetic trait passed down through the generations and exemplified in at least a couple of my mother's siblings. My mother was as genuine an example of what the church teaches that a Christian is supposed to be as I ever knew. She kept an array of pictures beside her bed of the people she was committed to praying for, and she arose early each morning, spent an hour or so on her knees in spite of her phlebitic legs praying for each one of these people in turn. This was done in private, and most people never knew that this was her daily habit. I'm confident that through the centuries there have been millions of genuinely loving people like this who professed to be Christians and who would have claimed that their behavior came from their faith.

However, this strong caveat: I'm also confident that there have been multiplied millions of people down through the centuries who were genuinely loving, kind, helping individuals who belonged to other religions than Christianity, or to no religion.

There is no evidence that religion, however pure, makes people good. There is plenty of evidence that religion makes some GOOD people do TERRIBLE things!

Let's return to the end of the Dark Ages and the beginning of the Protestant Reformation. It is impossible to say exactly when the Protestant Reformation against the Roman Catholic Church began. It is often dated from 1517 when Martin Luther nailed his 95 theses on the door of the church at Wittenberg. But it had many precursors in the two centuries before Luther. One was John Wycliffe of England, who was one of the first to insist that the Bible was the only authentic source of religious belief and should be translated into the language of the common people. So translate it he did, along with the help of several of his followers, in the latter part of the 14th Century. He also criticized the Catholic Church for its ostentatious wealth, which didn't win him any friends among the powerful in the church. He managed to die before the church got around to executing him, but he was declared a heretic after his death, his bones were dug up, burned, and his ashes scattered in the river, as if that made any difference to the dead Wycliffe.

Another forerunner of the Reformation was Jan Hus, a 15th Century Czech Catholic clergyman who followed Wickliffe's contention that the Bible should be able to be read by common people. He was not as fortunate as Wycliffe in that the church succeeded in having him declared a heretic, tried him in the German town of Constance, and burned him at the stake in 1415. It is said that just before the bundle of straw and stick which would burn him alive was lighted, Hus predicted that within one hundred years a reformer would arise who would be able to resist the power of the Catholic Church. Almost exactly one hundred years later Martin Luther publicized his 95 criticisms of the church.

Although Martin Luther was one of my heroes when I was in the Christian ministry because of his willingness to follow the dictates of his conscience no matter what the consequences for his career, and I still have significant admiration for him, he was not much better at accepting people with beliefs which differed from his than the Catholic Church had been. He is particularly noted for his polemics against the Jews, which have been credited by some for forming the philosophical basis for Hitler's pogroms against European Jews, resulting in six million deaths which Hitler claimed was done in the service of his church. Luther published a book in 1543 in which he advocated burning Jewish synagogues and schools for the "honor of our Lord." He also claimed that if he had the power, he would assemble all the Jewish leaders and threaten them with having their tongues cut off at the root if they did not accept that Jesus was the Messiah promised by their prophets.

Likewise many subsequent Protestant leaders who advocated for their own freedom to dissent from orthodox beliefs were not at all open to allowing others the same freedom if they had the power to control them. Such was the case when John Calvin, revered as the founder of the Presbyterian brand of protestant Christianity, would not allow Michael Servetus to disagree with him on his interpretation of the "holy Trinity" and when he had lured Servetus to come to Geneva, had him burned at the stake. Similar executions at the hands of protestant reformers occurred with other reformers like Ulrich Zwingli, John Tyndale, and Felix Manz, to name just a few.

It is estimated that throughout the entire history of

the Christian church seventy million people were killed for reasons of their religious beliefs. Only a small number of these were early martyrs during the first centuries before Christianity became the official state religion of the Roman Empire. The rest were killed by those who claimed to believe that Jesus was the Son of God sent to save mankind, but who would not allow other people to believe a different version of the same faith.

The claim by today's protestant Christians that the atrocities perpetrated by the church throughout history were primarily due to the usurpation of the "true" church by power-crazed prelates of the Roman Catholic Church is simply not substantiated by history. Protestants were obviously just as capable of persecuting and executing believers whose faith differed from their own as were the representatives of the church during the Dark Ages. However, the protestant persecution was much shorter lived because of the concomitant appearance in human history of the period known as the Renaissance.

The 16th Century is generally considered the beginning of the Renaissance when Polish cleric and scholar, Copernicus, published a book claiming a heliocentric view of the universe, meaning that the earth rotated around the sun, not the other way around. Remarkably, his work did not create a huge stir in the church until after his death, when it was roundly condemned, and Copernicus died still in the good graces of the church. A few decades later an Italian scientist, Galileo, confirmed Copernicus' findings with the advent of new and powerful telescopes, but he was not as fortunate of Copernicus. Galileo was subjected to house arrest for the rest of his life and forbidden to publish any more of such seditious works which contradicted "Holy Scripture." However, the scientific revolution had begun, and there was no stopping it. Developing scientific theories would go on to contradict almost everything about the Bronze Age understanding of reality during which standard Christian theology was instituted, including the demon-based view of the cause of illness, the idea that the matter consisted of the four "elements" of earth, fire, air, and water, the idea that the body was filled with the four humours of black bile, yellow bile, phlegm, and blood, and all sorts of attempts to understand the real world which were inaccurate, based upon the scientific ignorance of the time in which the Bible was written. The church would fight valiantly against these new scientific discoveries, but it would eventually lose.

It is worth noting that today's ongoing controversy between fundamentalist Christians and the idea of evolution is simply the most recent attempt by the church to squelch scientific information in favor of the Bronze Age view presented in the Bible. This squabble over teaching Creationism, or Intelligent Design, in the school system as an alternative to Darwin's theory of evolution will almost surely be looked upon by subsequent historians in much the same way we look at the Catholic Church's attempt to keep the Copernican theory of heliocentrism from being taught. Fundamentalist believers are on the wrong side of history, and scientific inquiry will ultimately prevail.

In relatively modern times the church, both Protestant and Catholic, has taken a strong stand on issues which most modern church members are now embarrassed to admit. The church was one of the most strident advocates for slavery in the South in the days before the Civil War. Many church members, both clerics and lay people, based their arguments for the institution of slavery on the Bible, where one can indeed find support for this horrible atrocity. In fact, the historical split among Baptists in this country into Southern Baptists and American Baptists was originally based on the issue of slavery. Most Southern Baptists I know wish that were not the case and try to claim that the main differences between the two groups had to do with evangelism. That is not at all what the facts reveal.

A strong case can be made that the worst atrocities committed during World War II were based on religion. A review of the writings and speeches of Hitler reveal that not only did he feel ordained by God to take over as much of the world as he could manage, but he was also quite clear that Jews deserved to be exterminated because they were agents of the devil, else they would have become Christians. And there is no denying that Hitler's Third Reich had the blessing of the Vatican.

So let's come down to even more recent years where the astonishing number of lawsuits against clergy and other church leaders for engaging in indefensible sexual predation against members of their own flocks has shocked the world. A significant number of these cases involve supposedly celibate priests of the Catholic Church and pedophilia toward children under their direct supervision, an absolutely unconscionable kind of behavior. However, an equally large number of cases of clear wrongdoing involve Protestant clergy and other church leaders. FREETHOUGHT TODAY, a publication of the Freedom From Religion Foundation, includes two entire pages each month called Black

Collar Crime Blotter, in which the names and alleged offenses of church personnel are detailed. It makes for depressing reading, as well as for a sense of outrage. I'm sure such inappropriate behaviors have gone on throughout the centuries, but they are only being brought to the public's attention in these days of relative greater freedom from religion's stranglehold.

This very brief summary of the history of the Christian church is meant only to illustrate what seems to me to be undeniable fact: namely, that the church cannot possibly have been the intention of any creator of the universe, for to claim otherwise is to assume that an omniscient, omnipotent God is incompetent or sadistic, or to assume with most of the founding fathers of our own government, who were Deists in the main, that if there were a God who formed the universe, He left it fail or succeed on its own -- or to assume that the Christian God is the creation of man, not the other way around.

So then, what about today's churches and all the people whose lives are oriented around them?

Before I make my radical suggestion of what I would like to see happen, let me say a bit more about the positive side of the church's history. Without a doubt, the Christian church has been responsible for many things of outstanding benefit to humanity. Architecture, art, music, educational institutions, hospitals, literature -- the list of its contributions to humanity is not endless, but it is exceedingly long. And society would indeed be greatly impoverished without these contributions which are a part and parcel of our culture. I have to believe that if the church hadn't existed, these contributions would likely have been significantly different, but would likely still have been made. Nonetheless, let's give credit where credit is due and admit that Michelangelo's Sistine Chapel and Handel's Messiah are among artistic human beings' greatest contributions.

Let me also say that a huge number of the members of traditional churches today belong to their churches for reasons other than a deep understanding of and commitment to the theology that is preached from their pulpits. They belong to their churches because it is the thing to do, because they want to help make the world a better place, and because they believe in honesty and justice and even mercy, within limits. My experience as a Southern Baptist minister convinces me that most church members have no idea about many of the things discussed in this chapter, have no idea how the Bible came to be, and have not even considered an alternative way of living which doesn't include the church. How else would society be moral, they think, without the church?

As I said to begin this chapter, these people cannot imagine their own lives without their local congregations.

So what would I suggest, since these church members are not about to give up their faith, leave the church en masse, and become reluctant atheists like me?

What I sincerely wish is that the church could give up its devotion to a theology which poses major problems for the integruous, intelligent believer and concentrate on doing what they claim was the primary purpose of Jesus, namely feeding the hungry, clothing the destitute, providing sustenance for those weakest among us who aren't able to cope because of the hand they have been dealt.

There is no question that there is a terrible amount of inequality inherent in the world. It simply is not true that "all men are created equal", however much our founding fathers may have wished it to be. The powerful feed off the powerless, and it was ever thus. The church could make its primary mission the effort to ameliorate some of that inequality and make life on this side of the grave not quite so grave for so many of earth's inhabitants.

I'd like to see the church begin to use the majority of its monies and energies in humanistic enterprises, not just a small portion of its resources. Approximately ninety percent of church funds are now used in maintaining the institution, with the other ten percent divided between trying to gain new members and just plain helping people. I'd like to see this proportion completely reversed with almost all donated funds used directly to help people. Some of the more enlightened churches are trying to move in this direction, but it is a very small percentage of churches, and it includes virtually none of the so-called "evangelical" groups whose main purpose remains to save souls from a nonexistent eternity of hell.

I'd like to see churches become more genuinely accepting of people who are different from the majority, like homosexuals, and grant them all the privileges and responsibilities of heterosexuals to marry, to adopt children, to serve their country. Again, some of the more progressive churches are moving in that direction, but the number is still very small.

In short, I'd like to see good church people outgrow the fairy tales they were taught as youths and engage in doing good for the sake of doing good, not to gain heavenly approval for doing so.

In point of fact, what I'm describing is very much like what the UU church has been about for as long as I can remember. As much as I respect the UU denomination for its intelligent stance on most issues, the reality is that the UU church has had a very hard time appealing to a significant number of people. So far as I can tell, its membership is not growing, whereas emotion-driven congregations all across the country are growing by leaps and bounds.

So I don't think that many churches are likely to move in the direction of a more accepting, genuinely caring family without all the trappings of the mythology of being saved by the blood of Jesus. And I must confess, if it did, the church might just die out because it would no longer have the promise of a life after death to provide impetus to its call for members. And it would no longer offer the comforting assurance that God has a plan for each life, and that everything will work out according to God's plan in the final analysis.

I understand very well the power of the desire to believe that the grave is not the end and that God is in charge of what happens in the world.

It is a very comforting thought.

The only problem is: THERE IS NO ULTIMATE COMFORT IN A LIE!

JESUS AS PAUL BUNYAN

Paul Bunyan was a delightful, mythical character who was, quite literally, bigger than life. He was a legendary woodsman of unbelievable size, strength and courage, who had a companion blue ox named Babe, also much bigger than life.

The Bunyan character first appeared in a story by James MacGillivray in 1906. Several northern states claim to be the birthplace of Paul Bunyan, and there are statues and theme parks based on the legend in many states from Maine to Oregon.

As the story spread, the tall tales got bigger and bigger. Those were the days when logging ruled the day in the heavily-forested northern states, and stories of giant woodsmen of superhuman strength were common. All these stories contributed to the Paul Bunyan legend.

But everybody knows that these fabulous stories are just that: they are stories, not history. There are those who think that a Canadian logger named Fournier, who was an extremely large man with superior strength, formed the basis for the Paul

Bunyan legend. As the legend grew and spread across the country, people loved telling the tall tales and adding their own embellishments to the stories. There were even some people, usually in isolated places with little educational opportunity, who claimed to believe that Paul Bunyan was a real historical person, even if they acknowledged that the stories about him had been "puffed up" a bit.

Today, is there anyone who would claim that the Paul Bunyan of legend really lived and walked tall through the north woods?

Probably not. Why? Because we know how such stories get started, passed on, and embellished with each re-telling. And because no one has told us that believing the Paul Bunyan stories is essential to living a meaningful life in this world and having the promise of a life to come beyond the grave.

So what does that have to do with Jesus? A lot, actually. But first, let's turn to what true believers think they know about Jesus.

All "born again" believers are certain that they know Jesus. They have read about Jesus in their Bibles, they have heard about Jesus in their churches, and they are certain that Jesus has forgiven them their sins and taken up residence in their hearts.

The Jesus that they think they know is a bigger-than-life personage who must have been incredibly magnetic and persuasive, the very definition of the word "charismatic". People of faith talk about loving Jesus in a way they don't talk of loving anyone else in history whom they've never actually met.

I know, I know, committed Christians are incensed at the very suggestion that they haven't actually met Jesus. They will argue vehemently that they have indeed met Jesus, that they know him intimately and are closer to him than to their dearest friend. "O, how I love Jesus because he first loved me" says the familiar gospel song.

How can they love someone whom they have never met in the flesh? It's all a part of the emotional experience that underlies all religion. For true believers, the emotions are the reality, and they are absolutely certain that they know Jesus.

But just who is this Jesus that Christians are so sure they know?

True believers, again, will say that Jesus was the one individual in history who divided recorded history into two parts -- BC (before Christ) and AD (Anno Domini, in the year of our Lord). And they are right. Our yearly calendar which claims that this is the year 2010 AD, as I write this, means 2010 years after the (supposed) birth of Jesus and is the result of the adoption of a standard calendar by most of the Western world in relatively recent history.

If you haven't followed the dating system closely or read the history of how our current calendar came into being, you might assume that Jesus' birth had such an immediate impact on the world that countries began dating their calendars from his birth in the early centuries. You would be wrong.

The actual history of our current calendar, known officially as the Gregorian calendar, dates back to 1582 when it was authorized by Pope Gregory XIII. However, it is based on the Julian calendar which was adopted during the reign of Julius Caesar, half a century before the reported birth, life and death of Jesus. The Roman calendar in use during the time of Julius Caesar's reign was quite confusing. Not only did

Roman emperors before Julius regularly change the number of days in a month in order to make themselves look better, but the calendar year was not in sync with the solar year. Julius Caesar changed that with his Julian calendar, which included a leap year every four years and helped sync the calendar with the solar year, though not completely accurately.

Early believers were in no sense dominant during the first several centuries AD, or what is now known as the Common Era (CE). They were either ignored, ridiculed, or persecuted in those days, and no one would have considered re-dating the calendar from the birth of Jesus. It wasn't until more than three hundred years after the reported birth of Jesus that the Roman Emperor Constantine decided not only to become a Christian, but, probably mostly for political reasons, also abolished all persecution of Christians and returned to them their property, taken during the reign of Diocletian. Eventually, Constantine declared all the Roman Empire to be officially Christian, including the forced baptism of his troops by marching them through a river en masse, according to some reports. Thus, he created what became known as the Holy Roman Empire in which the Catholic Church and its Papacy were given enormous power.

Constantine is considered a saint by the Roman Catholic tradition, and he certainly did yeoman service to the Church with his edicts regarding Christianity. However, he was ruthless and power-driven. This ruthlessness eventuated in his having one of his sons and his wife both executed, hardly the acts of a "born again" person who was a "new creation in Christ"!

It was around the 8th Century CE (AD) that the dating of the calendar began to be from the supposed date of Jesus' birth. Ironically, even that was mathematically off by a half dozen years, with most experts agreeing that the actual date for Jesus' birth (if indeed someone named Jesus was an actual historical person) was perhaps 5 to 7 BCE (BC). And the current Gregorian calendar was not proposed until the 14th century CE (AD), and not universally adopted until relatively recent times.

But a believer can still say that whenever it happened, the fact that our current calendar dates from the time of Jesus proves absolutely that Jesus was the most important personage to ever walk the earth.

Doesn't it?

Well, it certainly indicates the influence that religion has had on the world. But it no more proves that Jesus was God in the flesh than the Salem witch trials proved that witches exist and should be killed. Or than the pyramids of Egypt, marvelous structures for their day, prove that the pharaohs were chosen to rule by the sun god.

There is no doubt that the "story" of the life and death of Jesus has had unprecedented influence on the history of the world. How much of that story is likely to be accurate?

As we will discuss in the chapter on the Bible, we do not have a single actual manuscript of any part of our current Bible, either Old or New Testament. And what copies of copies of the New Testament books that do exist do not even pretend to be history of the life of Jesus. What we have are documents of faith. The main source of what we think we know about Jesus comes from the four Gospels of the Bible's New Testament: Matthew, Mark, Luke, and John. Three of these, Matthew, Mark and Luke, give an account similar enough to each other that they are called the Synoptic Gospels, meaning "seeing with the same eye". There are many passages in these three accounts of Jesus' life which are almost identical, leading to the assumption that Mark was written first, with Matthew and Luke copying Mark, or that all three were partly based on an earlier document which is referred to as "Q" from a German word meaning "source". However, it must be noted that even though many passages are similar, there are significant discrepancies even in these "synoptic" gospels, a strange occurrence if these accounts are based on anything like accurate history.

The fourth gospel, John, is believed by scholars to have been written several decades later, at least one hundred years after the supposed birth of Jesus, and it has many unique passages which aren't to be found anywhere else. Some of the most powerful stories about Jesus are found only in John, like the one about his pardon of the woman about to be stoned for adultery, as well as some of the more familiar verses like John 3:16, which evangelicals are very zealous about promoting.

We have no idea who the actual authors of the gospel accounts were. The familiar names attached to them were added later. Only two of them, Matthew and John, are listed among the twelve apostles and thus claimed by promoters of the faith to have been actual eyewitnesses to any of the events being described. The other two author names attached to their gospels, Mark and Luke, are never reported to have met Jesus in the flesh, as indeed the other most prolific New Testament writer, Paul, did not. Almost all scholars agree that Mark was the first gospel to be written, but at the very earliest it was penned at least forty years after Jesus' reported death. It had to be based on an oral tradition that had been passed down over these years, since whoever Mark (if that was indeed the author's name) was, he could not have known first hand about the things he wrote.

But all these accounts, even if they were all to agree, which they don't, are still not histories. They are "gospels". The word "gospel" is a translation from the Greek of a word which meant "to evangelize". Thus, the recorded stories we have had through the centuries about Jesus were written for one clear and stated purpose: to convince people that Jesus was God become flesh. There was not even the slightest indication that they were meant to be objective. They were written by believers whose intention was to help other people become believers.

Throughout the history of the Common Era there have been attempts to discover just how much of the gospel story of the life, death and resurrection of Jesus is likely to be accurate. This is generally referred to as the quest for the historical Jesus, also the title of a book by Albert Schweitzer. Early on there was disagreement about many of the reported details of the Jesus story. There were several other "gospels" written about Jesus, which early church leaders arbitrarily decided were not authentic and should not be included in the Bible. Some of these included stories about the infant Jesus performing miracles and, in one instance, striking a temple teacher dead because he tried to correct the child Jesus.

There were also conflicting opinions about when, if, and how Jesus actually became one with God. The Council of Nicaea in 325 CE was called by the Emperor Constantine I to try to decide among conflicting opinions whether Jesus was one with God or simply the representative of God. Suffice it to say there was anything but unanimity among believers, to say nothing of the varying opinions among historians who have attempted to sort through the religious traditions to discover what may have been the historical facts.

Some current scholars have concluded that the entire Jesus story may have been concocted from whole cloth, with no actual historical person on whom the story was based. There is certainly some logical support for this idea. There was a history of religions based on virgin births of god-figures throughout the region long before the story of Jesus and of sacrificial saviors who rose from the dead. There is the possibility of numerology being involved in the fact that Jesus is reported to have chosen "twelve" apostles, just like the twelve months of the year and the twelve tribes of Israel. And there is the undeniable fact that essentially nothing is reported in the surviving gospels about the details of Jesus' life before he began his messianic ministry, save the one story about his confounding the religious professionals in the temple when he was twelve, again the special number.

One of the pieces of evidence against the historicity of the Jesus story is that there is essentially no writing from secular historians of the time to corroborate the story. I was taught in seminary that the most powerful non-Christian evidence for the life of Jesus was to be found in the writings of a Jewish historian named Josephus. However, further study on my own revealed that virtually no one except fundamentalist Christians believe that the brief mention of Jesus in Josephus' Antiquities of the Jews was part of the original text, but that it was added later by believers in order to bolster their claims about Jesus.

It seems more than passing strange that with all the influence that the religion which grew up around Jesus has had on history, no one who lived at the same time and who was not a believer and an evangelist for the story saw fit to mention that such a person even existed. We know lots about secular rulers of that day, even a fair amount about Jewish leaders of the time, but not one word from someone without an axe to grind about this person on whose story the calendar was divided into before and after.

More than passing strange!

The most familiar collection of the supposed teachings of Jesus is found in what is called the Sermon on the Mount. It is found in Matthew 5, 6, and 7, and it is found only in Matthew. Although the other three gospels contain some reported teachings of Jesus which are similar to some of the content of the Sermon on the Mount, none of them mentions that this event occurred.

More than passing strange!

Most reputable Biblical scholars conclude that whoever wrote the Gospel of Matthew put together teachings which Jesus may have offered during his brief ministry, as well as teachings of others during that same time, and concocted the story about Jesus delivering this sermon all at one time. There are some beautiful passages in this sermon, along with some very troubling stuff. For instance, the command to pluck out your eyeball if it should be guilty of offense is extremely difficult for Biblical literalists!

And many of the suggestions Jesus is reported to have made, like "Take no thought for tomorrow, for sufficient unto the day is the evil thereof", may have been based on the assumption that early believers thought the end of the world was near. Jesus himself is reported to have encouraged this belief with his claim that many of those who heard his voice would not see death but would be around for the "return of the Son of Man in his glory."

I don't know whether there was a Jesus who said this or not. But I know that throughout the 2000 or so years since then, thousands of faithful believers have been expecting the world to come to an end during their lifetimes. And many of them have rearranged their lives on this false premise, with terribly damaging consequences. I know many people today who absolutely believe that the "rapture", or second-coming of Jesus, will occur before they die. Many of them are good, sincere people of integrity who base their plans for the future on this belief.

I cannot help thinking how tragic that such valuable human potential is being wasted on such a spurious idea.

I must confess that I remain basically agnostic about how much, if any, of the story of Jesus is actual history. I seriously doubt that we will ever be able to conclusively determine a factual answer to this quandary. And it is essentially irrelevant. If there is no over-arching, all-powerful, all-loving God in charge of the universe and of eternity, which I'm convinced is what scientific and logical evidence shows, it doesn't matter if a story about someone whose followers claimed that he was God become flesh is based on some grain of historical fact or is a complete invention during a religiously-oriented time of humanity's existence.

However, I'll give you my best guess. It makes sense to me that there may actually have been a historic figure named Jesus who, well into his adulthood, decided that he was destined to become an itinerant prophet and began going about the countryside preaching a fairly radical brand of faith. If so, my hunch is that he made this decision partly because he was aware that his was an unusually magnetic kind of personality and that he could probably inspire a lot of people to believe his teachings and follow his leadership. And he may well have gotten into hot water with the professional religionists of his day, such that they conspired to have him executed. I doubt seriously that he thought he was God or the Son of God. Many Biblical passages support this notion with Jesus' reported most common reference to himself as the "son of man", not "son of God."

In any event, whether there was an actual historical Jesus or not, it is all but certain that the stories about Jesus grew in much the same way that the stories about the mythical Paul Bunyan grew after this super-human character was introduced in the early 20th Century.

Not only do human beings like tall tales, we also tend to want our heroes to be bigger than life. We've done it in recent history with such actual people as George Washington, Daniel Boone, Davy Crockett, and Abraham Lincoln. If this kind of "writing up" of a hero in relatively sophisticated modern times can occur so easily, it is certainly understandable that this happened in spades in the time of the reported historical Jesus. Thus, the miracles which Jesus supposedly performed were surely examples of "writing up" the hero. Walking on water, calming the sea, turning water into wine, raising Lazarus from the dead, curing leprosy by commanding the demons which caused it to enter a herd of swine -- all these are like the stories of George Washington cutting down the cherry tree and being unable to lie about it and Paul Bunyan having a breakfast table several miles long because of his huge appetite.

Likewise, the story of the virgin birth of Jesus, of the journey of the magi who followed a mysterious star, of the appearance to shepherds of angels to announce Jesus' magical birth, of his family's flight into Egypt because of Herod's edict to kill all the infants in the region who might grow up to challenge his rule, and most of all, of Jesus' bodily resurrection after his crucifixion and ascent into heaven some weeks later -- all these stories are best understood as believers' additions to the story of a sincere, well-intentioned, magnetic personality to make him into "God become flesh" to redeem mankind.

How do I know? Well, I don't absolutely know, and you are free to choose another interpretation if you wish. But as one who spent half a lifetime trying to make sense of the mythology I was taught from childhood and not being able to do so, I am willing to bet my life on it.

This leads me to a brief comment on Pascal's Wager, which some people still bring up when they find out that I'm now comfortable calling myself an atheist. A seventeenth century French mathematician, Blaise Pascal, argued that even though logic might lead one to the conclusion that there is no God, to trust that logic would be a mistake. For if one believes in God and is wrong, he simply experiences non-existence after death just as the atheist does, but if he is right, he experiences life eternal in heaven. Whereas if one doesn't believe in God and is wrong, he experiences eternal punishment. This is commonly referred to as Pascal's Wager.

There are many ways in which this wager may be shown to be silly, including that the true God may not be the Christian God at all, but some other God like Vishnu, or Ra, or the Pleiades. In this case belief in the Christian God would be tantamount to eternal punishment because you believed in the wrong God. Or the idea that there is a God, but He deliberately allowed the growth of religious myth so that only those who could see through the myth would be rewarded with eternal life.

But my main reason for being willing to bet against Pascal is that I have tried as valiantly as I could to be able to believe what the Christian religion teaches, but I simply am not able to do so. It just doesn't make sense. It is full of holes. And the history of the Christian religion has not made the world a better place, in the main, but has instead contributed to man's inhumanity to man.

I am committed to trying to help make the world a better place, to giving up the infighting about who has the inside corner on truth, and to living my life with as much integrity as I know how to do.

If, perchance, there should be a God and an afterlife, which I think is highly unlikely, I'll take my chances on the fairness of the judgment of such a being to put my pitiful little struggle in perspective and deal with me accordingly.

The myth of Paul Bunyan makes a good story, as does the story of Jesus of Nazareth.

But neither story stands up to factual scrutiny or gives us a clue about the meaning of life.

For that, we have brains.

FAITH: BELIEVING WITHOUT EVIDENCE

Faith.

An emotion-laden word, both in content and context. It literally means giving credence to something (an idea, a story, a concept) for which there is little, if any, empirical evidence.

Even the author of the Biblical book of Hebrews acknowledged that faith is non-empirical when, in his exhortation praising faith, he begins with the words, "Now faith is the substance of things hoped for, the evidence of things not seen." (Hebrews 11:1) If you were hearing these words for the first time, you would immediately know that they make no sense; things only "hoped for" have no substance whatsoever, and things "not seen" provide zero visual evidence.

So faith is no more solid than a gambler's fervent belief that this time the dice will come up in his favor, a belief fostered by nothing more than a desire that it should be so.

When most people talk about their own religious faith, they are referring to doctrines about supernatural propositions and stories established as the "truth" in their religious community. But at an emotional level they are alluding to a commitment they have made to be good, upright people, to be living in accord with what they understand to be just, fair, even grace-bestowing. To question their faith is tantamount to demeaning their morality, their ethics, their understanding of the difference between good and evil.

I want to be crystal clear that the last thing I intend is to criticize people of faith, many of whom are like the salt of the earth in their attempt to make the world a better place. I do not mean to critique people of faith; I do mean to critique the faith of the people.

It is commonplace for religious skeptics like me to accord respect for someone's faith, however much we may disagree with it.

For example: "Oh, you don't eat meat on Fridays because it's against your faith? Well, if that's your faith, I respect that." Or, "God would be upset with you if you cut your hair (or trimmed your beard, or rode in a motorized vehicle, or failed to say a blessing before a meal). Since that's your faith, I respect that."

That is the position I once took, knowing first-hand what it was like to believe totally in what I had been taught from my youth. I remember when I gave up playing first chair in the clarinet section of my high school band because I refused to appear at a band concert on a Wednesday night, which was prayer meeting night at my church. I dare not have missed prayer meeting because that is what you did on Wednesday nights in that church tradition if you were a good Christian. For my band instructor to think I could go against those principles was an assault on my entire life-system.

However, I am now committed to the position that

while everyone is free to believe anything he/she chooses, however ridiculous I may think it is, I am no longer willing to fall into the politically-correct trap of according respect, either implicit or explicit, to beliefs I hold to be manifestly senseless.

Let's take an extreme example to make the point. Suppose someone said that since Jesus is reported to have ridden triumphantly into Jerusalem on a donkey, with palm leaves being strewn along his path, his faith said he should never ride a donkey lest he be guilty of trying to put himself on a par with "his Lord" and never cut down a palm tree since to do so would besmirch the name of Jesus. I made up this example from whole cloth, simply trying to find the silliest article of faith imaginable, and I'm assuming that this particular belief does not actually exist in the real world.

Now, should we say in this instance, "Since that's your faith, I respect that and will be sure I never offend you by riding a donkey or cutting down a palm tree in your presence?" Hardly! Instead, we would be justified in saying, "Believe that if you wish, but I think it's downright stupid."

Well, maybe we wouldn't say that unless we had a long-term relationship with the person and this irrational belief significantly affected our lives in some way. But we would surely think it.

Let's make it even more ridiculous. Suppose someone said he believed in a real Easter bunny, a real tooth fairy, a real Santa Claus, and this someone was an otherwise competent adult who showed no other evidence of mental illness. Wouldn't you be thunderstruck? Wouldn't you think this is ridiculous in the extreme and not even come close to according respect to that belief system?

I certainly would. I think most intelligent people would. And you'd probably feel no guilt or emotional discomfort in doing so because the belief system is so patently absurd that no mature, sane person you know would hold it.

Ah, there's the rub. If the belief system is one which lots of people hold or one to which you've grown accustomed, it becomes much harder to look at it dispassionately and analyze whether it makes any logical sense. One tends to feel guilty attacking someone else's belief system. However, the further away from your own personal experience, the easier it is to do without undue anxiety.

For instance, in this country most people have probably never seen a devout Buddhist turning a prayer wheel while uttering ritualistic phrases. Most of us have only seen such a thing on film. So do you think turning that prayer wheel has anything to do with living an ethical life or in some way makes the world a better place? I'll bet not. Since the faith of some Buddhists does hold that this activity is significant, I certainly wouldn't try to deny them the right to do it. I just think the energy involved in doing that could be better placed. And I wouldn't hesitate saying so under the right conditions.

Let's take a more serious example, one closer to home. A depressed mother of several children admitted to drowning all of them in order to keep them from the sinful influences of the secular world. She said she was sure she was doing God's will. Should we accord this faith system respect? Surely not!

Now, let's take a much more common example which has equally serious consequences because of its ubiquity. People of faith are told by their leaders to turn their lives over to God and that, after doing so, they never have to be responsible for any decision. God will guide them if they simply pray for God's will to be done. But on what basis do they determine God's will? On the basis of their emotions, pure and simple. Ask anyone of this persuasion how he knows whether he's doing God's will, and the answer is that he has this feeling deep inside which convinces him of it.

Let's face it: emotions are an inadequate reason for choosing one path over another, being wrong as often as being right.

Feelings are a good gift, but a poor guide!

Would it surprise you to know that many of the currently accepted articles of Christian faith were anything but universally accepted in the early years of Christianity? Take the idea, central to church doctrine, that Jesus was God become flesh, not just the representative of God. You may think that this "truth" was accepted by all believers from the beginning of the Christian religion, but that is not the case. It was not until three hundred years or so after Jesus' reported crucifixion and resurrection that the doctrine of the trinity, meaning that the one true God has three separate manifestations, became codified as "inspired truth." Just to put that into perspective, that's longer than the United States has been a country!

And how did this "truth" become established? It was voted on.

I won't bore you with details regarding the numerous "Councils" which were held during the first centuries of the Christian religion, which councils set themselves to the task of deciding what was "truth" and what wasn't. The reason these meetings were called was that there was nothing approaching agreement on the details of what Christians were supposed to believe. It isn't entirely clear just how the people who made up these councils were chosen, but let's assume that they were representative of the various communities of Christians in that part of the world. What is clear is that the council meetings were anything but serene and were characterized by intense disagreements among the participants.

So after lots of debate pro and con in these councils, final decisions about what Christians should believe were voted on. The people who were most persuasive carried the day, and the ones who were outvoted went back to their communities to lick their wounds and to hope to fight another day. Often the minority view continued in a local community for many long years, all the while being characterized as heretical by those who had won the vote in the particular council meeting.

If the story about the God of the universe (the universe, mind you, not just the rather insignificant little ball of rock, dirt and water we call home, which is just one of multiplied billions of such balls in the universe) deciding to become flesh on this earth in order to rescue his prize creation were really true, does it make sense to you that it would be done in such a way that people who lived in or near that time would have trouble agreeing about what had happened and what it meant? That they would have to convene council meetings over several centuries to vote on what was true and what wasn't? I mean, come on -- does that really make sense to you? Wouldn't you think that the all-powerful, all-knowing God of the universe could have made a better job of it than that?

Of course, true believers will say that this description of how the tenets of the Christian faith came to be standard doctrine is not at all the way it happened. They will contend that I'm making it sound all too human and subject to human error and manipulation.

Well, the fact is that it was indeed a very human process with lots of disagreement among the religious leaders of the day who engaged in the process of voting on what should be believed and what shouldn't. Today's "true believers" who refuse to acknowledge this history are guilty of putting halos around these early believers and their deliberations. It's an understandable mistake, but it is a mistake nonetheless.

It is somewhat on the same order as what we Americans are prone to do about the history of the founding of our country. We tend to revere our founding fathers almost as if they were a special order of human being, glossing over or totally ignoring the fact that not only were they products of their time, but they were also subject to the same human frailties as today's citizens. And our country's history is only a couple of hundred years old, when people had a much more advanced ability to record what actually happened than was true in the ancient times when the Christian religion was being created.

It's no wonder that well-meaning, intelligent people, who in other areas of their lives depend upon evidence before accepting something as accurate, can be found espousing the most outrageous claims which they have been taught in their particular brand of faith.

Let's explore a bit further the idea that we look at incredible claims about reported events which took place in a time long ago in a different way than we do similar events which occur today.

Remember the dramatic case of the Heaven's Gate cult which resulted in a mass suicide of 39 people in 1997? This small cult which never numbered more than one hundred people was founded by one Marshall Herff Applewhite, the son of an itinerant Presbyterian minister. Applewhite had begun his career as a talented musician, a singer with the Houston Grand Opera, and a university professor, only to be forced to resign his position because of an alleged sexual affair with a male student. Subsequently, while a patient in a psychiatric hospital he met and teamed up with a nurse with psychic leanings named Bonnie, and together they began roaming the country, formulating their "special revelation," and gathering followers who left their families to become a part of this new cult. They decided they were the second coming of Christ, as well as the two witnesses to the Apocalypse described in the Biblical book of Revelation, and took on new names, the last of which were Do and Ti, after the first and last syllables in the musical scale.

After wandering for several years in order to keep families members from being able to locate loved ones who had joined the group, the Heaven's Gate group settled in San Diego to await word about when they would be transported to the "next level" of existence. They followed strict codes of conduct prescribed by Do and Ti, including absolutely no sexual thoughts or behaviors. Some of the males had themselves surgically castrated in order to comply with this regimen. The group settled on the name Heaven's Gate to describe their belief that they were entrusted with important information about how to exit this world for a better one beyond. When the Hale-Bopp comet was discovered, Applewhite decided that this was their cue to depart this existence and engineered a mass suicide complete with videotapes of each of the members just before the ritualized drinking of Phenobarbital mixed with vodka.

It is a bizarre story!

Now, what are the chances that you believe that this group was actually following a divine revelation and that God intended that they should behave this way?

I'll hazard a guess that the chances are slim to none!

Why?

Because it happened in modern times when we are able to recognize that the behavior doesn't make sense or square with any view of reality that we hold to be rational.

Actually, the story is no more bizarre than many of the ones told in the Bible, which stories are standard theology for most believers. Like the stories of Moses and the burning bush, of the parting of the Red Sea, of the walls of Jericho tumbling down, of Enoch (Methuselah's father) being bodily transported to heaven without dying, and dozens of other bizarre stories in the Bible's Old Testament. Or of stories about Jesus and his disciples in the New Testament, like the one about raising Lazarus from the dead, or turning water into wine, or causing demons to come out of a leper and enter a herd of swine, or of Jesus being resurrected from the dead, appearing to his disciples and then bodily ascending to heaven.

Why do believers accept the bizarre Bible stories as being divinely inspired and not the Heaven's Gate debacle? Because the stories that belong to their faith happened a long time ago, and they were taught them as credulous children. (Of course, not all religious believers heard and accepted these stories as children. But in the main, even if they were converted as adults, they entered a community of faith where the majority had accepted these beliefs as children and considered them off-limits to rational questioning.)

I submit that if the claims which make up the theology of the dominant religions of today had been presented to us as occurring in modern time, in the same way the details of the Heaven's Gate cult became known, that essentially no one in his/her right mind would believe any of them. Only a few pitiful people with emotional problems would give them any credence.

But the members of traditional religions are certainly not few in number, nor are they mostly pitiful folks with emotional problems.

My point exactly! They are able to suspend rational thought patterns because of the context in which these notions are presented -- a long history in which people have accepted bizarre beliefs about events in the distant past.

But there are even more powerful reasons that religion has continued to exert such influence on a large segment of the population of an educated, enlightened society like ours, and the most salient of those reasons are the following:

The fear of death and of what, if anything, lies beyond the grave

The need to belong

The psychological need to be right.

FEAR OF DEATH

So far as we know, human beings are the only creatures on earth which are able to contemplate the end of their lives. Other sentient creatures certainly witness death, and some, like the elephant, even appear to go through a grieving process when one of their own dies. It's possible that this may cause them to acknowledge their own mortality, but because they don't use verbal language that we can understand, we have no way of knowing whether that happens.

We human beings, however, clearly know that we're going to die, that our conscious existence as we have known it will come to an end. And although people differ in how much this reality concerns them, it's fair to say that virtually everyone struggles to find a way to accept his/her own mortality.

Death scares us. It puzzles us. It motivates us to try to find a way to keep from having to accept its finality.

Throughout human history people have invented ways to make themselves believe that death is not the end but is, instead, only a transition to another type of existence. We know this is true because of all the historical records which have been kept since writing became commonplace, and we know that belief in a life beyond death existed before the era of historical records because of the excavation of grave sites which include all sorts of artifacts buried with people in an apparent attempt to facilitate their existence in a life beyond the grave.

There is no way to know for sure, but it would certainly seem that the difficulty of accepting the finality of death was the very first human motivation for creating religious belief systems. All religions of which I'm aware, both primitive and current, have some sort of answer to the question of what happens beyond the grave. And that answer is NEVER that the grave is the end!

In all likelihood the grave is, in fact, the end. Not a transition to another life on a different plane. Not the beginning of either a life of eternal bliss or the beginning of a life of eternal suffering. Not the reunion of the deceased with those who have died previously or a rebirth into another earthly life either as another human being or as a different kind of creature, as reincarnation tenets would have people believe.

There is no credible evidence that death for human beings is anything different than what it is for every other creature -- the end of existence. Our bodies die and decay, including our brains where our personalities reside, and we don't "pass on" to anything else. Because there isn't anything else. It's over. The end. Finis. We cease to exist.

But, faithful critics argue, what if you're wrong, Mr. Smarty Pants, and there is life beyond the grave? Well, great! I'd be happy to be wrong. And I'll be happy to take my chances on being treated fairly, even with my history of religious skepticism, by whoever is in charge of a "life beyond the grave". The idea that an inscrutable Lord of the universe would condemn me to an eternal existence of punishment because I was unable, in spite of half a lifetime of trying, to believe in the tenets of the Christian faith, or any other faith for that matter, is just too unconscionable for words. I simply would not, could not in good conscience, live my life any differently if it should turn out that I'm wrong about death being final.

But, as I said, there is simply no credible evidence

that the grave is anything but the end, however much human beings may want to believe otherwise. And human beings as a whole certainly DO want to believe otherwise. In spades they want to believe otherwise. So we use euphemisms like "passing on", "going home", and "shedding this mortal coil" to avoid talking honestly about dying.

There is a story about the little boy whose cat died after being hit by a car while the boy was in school. Upon hearing about the accident, the lad asked where the cat was now. Not wanting to upset his son, the father told him that his cat had gone to be with Jesus. With much more candor than the parents could muster, the boy replied, "What in the world does Jesus want with a dead cat?"

I know it is really hard to wrap your mind around the idea of no longer existing. Most people in the developed world have no trouble acknowledging that we did not exist before we were born, (the major exception being Mormons who support the LDS doctrine that heaven is filled with millions of unborn souls which the faithful must assist in bringing to life), but it is still difficult to imagine no longer existing after death. I know that it is difficult because, although I accept that this is what the evidence suggests, I still am not able to imagine what non-existence is like. I have no fear of it -- why should one? -- but I simply cannot honestly say that I understand what that will be like or that I can imagine myself not existing.

I'm convinced that the most powerful reason religious faith still holds sway over otherwise intelligent, evidence-oriented people is the fact that all religions promise something beyond the grave.

NEED TO BELONG

Although human beings differ in how much people contact they need and in how important membership in a group is, it's safe to say that virtually everyone has some need to belong. I would hunch that this need to belong is in our genes, just as it is in the genes of all herd and/or den animals.

The church (or temple or mosque or other religious grouping) meets this need in spades. Whatever answer faithful church members give to the question about why they hold the faith they hold, the reality is that for a very large percentage of "believers" the principle reason they go to church is because of the sense of community they feel in doing so. From my own experience of having been raised in the church and from having spent twenty years as an active minister, I know for certain that this sense of belonging to a larger family group of like-minded people is a huge part of the reason that the church still appeals to so many people in this country.

Never underestimate the need to belong! It's a large part of the answer to why gangs appeal to kids in ghettos, why sororities/fraternities hold such sway in higher education, why service clubs like Rotary, Kiwanis, Lions, Elks, etc., become a major personal identity factor for millions of people. It's likely a very large factor in why tribal membership is so important to most Native Americans, as it is to less-developed tribal societies around the globe. There is obviously an incredible need to belong to a group which helps people feel comfortable with their own sense of identity.

I have not spent time with other cultures and their particular religious traditions, but everything I have read and what little actual contact I have had with people from those traditions leads me to believe that this same factor is present in spades in those other religions as well.

The power of this belonging factor is such that if other people who are a part of your religious community accept (or appear to accept) the tenets of the faith which defines the group, there isn't much incentive to question any of those tenets for yourself.

Or if you do question them, to keep quiet about it because all the others in your faith community are keeping quiet about any questions they might have as well. You don't want to rock the boat. You want to fit in. You want to belong.

Let's be brutally honest and also admit that in many cases membership in a particular church or religious tradition is a smart business, as well as social, move. Church membership tends to segregate itself along educational and class lines, and within those boundaries, being a member of a particular religious group is good business. It would likely be hard to get many church members to honestly admit this as a motivation, but only a fool could fail to see the connection.

When I first left the Baptist church, I joined a Unitarian-Universalist congregation. I did so because I could be a member of this group without compromising my basic rejection of the theistic tradition, as well as because I was accustomed to belonging to a church. I enjoyed much about my association with this grouping of mostly well-educated, ethical, caring human beings. The UU tradition, unlike virtually all other church traditions, is quite accepting of free-thinkers, agnostics, atheists -- and, interestingly, even of traditional theists, even though their numbers among UU members are not large. So I could be a member of this group with integrity, without compromising my inability to believe in the tenets of traditional Christian faith.

I filled the pulpit countless times as a UU, sang in many a UU choral group, and occasionally participated in re-writing some traditional hymns to make them palatable to a UU congregation. I was asked more than once whether I would consider becoming a UU minister. I must confess that had I known earlier in my ministerial career that one could be an atheist and still be a minister in the UU church, that is probably what I would have done.

However, after many years as a UU, I began to think that much of what went on in that organization was a waste of time, energy, and money. There is a joke among Unitarian-Universalists that the UU church is for people who no longer believe in God but who are not quite ready to give up going to church. Frankly, that is how it began to feel to me. I enjoyed much about the experience of being a UU, and if I were to belong to any religious group today, it would be to the UU church. The UU church is in many ways a wonderful organization, which does a lot of good in the world. I agree with its social consciousness, its acceptance of people of all stripes, its meritorious program of instruction for young people.

I simply no longer feel the need to belong to any religious organization.

However, I understand how strong the need to belong is. And I know that the strong sense of community which most people of faith feel in their church is a huge part of what keeps them from questioning various tenets of their faith which they might otherwise reject.

It is not by accident that church members refer to members of their congregation as "our church family." The church does, in fact, become like an extended family to its members. For many people being able to identify yourself as a member of a certain religious group is as important as being able to say what state and country holds your citizenship.

This leads to the third reason that intelligent people continue to hold on to beliefs for which there is little or no evidence. It is a psychological phenomenon which is as powerful as it is common.

NEED TO BE RIGHT

Let's discuss two aspects of this common need.

The first is the difficulty people have holding opinions which aren't consonant with prevailing views. Simply put, there is a strong human tendency to agree with the people around you.

Let me give you an example from a kind of psychological experiment which has been performed many times, with very consistent results. You have people in a group with the instructions to say which of two given lines is longer. Out of six people in the experiment, only one is a real subject; the rest are accomplices (usually referred to in experimental psychology as "stooges" because of the role they are playing) who are instructed with how to answer. Over several trials, the five stooges answer correctly about which line is longer, as does the actual experimental subject. Then comes a trial where the stooges all answer incorrectly about which line is longer. In a significantly large number of times, the actual subject, who has heard all the others answer incorrectly, also answers incorrectly. In post-experimental interviews when the subjects are asked why they answered the way they did, they essentially say that they thought the other line looked longer, but since everyone before them had seen it otherwise, they didn't want to go against the grain.

This kind of experiment clearly shows the strength of the need to agree with the group so as not to be wrong, even when one's own experience indicates that the group may be wrong. It doesn't turn out that way 100 percent of the time, but it is a very reliable outcome with a majority of people.

It is amazing how often people don't trust their own judgment. It helps to explain the popularity of such clearly bogus fields as astrology, tarot cards, palm reading, and the like.

But there is another psychological reason that people hold on to attitudes and/or beliefs which do not square with evidence, and it has to do with what happens inside our brains when there in inconsistency. This inconsistency, or cognitive dissonance, makes us uncomfortable, and we choose the least painful way to resolve the discomfort. Since it is seldom easy to admit being wrong, that's not the most common way to resolve the discomfort. What is much more common is to reinterpret the evidence to be consistent with a behavior we've already done or a stance we've already taken.

A simple example reveals the process. Let's say you have finally decided on which new car to purchase after evaluating several options. Immediately after making this decision, it's common to look for evidence that you have made the right choice. You notice negative things about the other possible choices you rejected and point them out, feeling comforted by the knowledge. You also ignore, or try to explain away, negative information about your own choice.

This phenomenon becomes even more powerful if you have been through a particularly arduous time in making this decision. Group leaders have long known that allegiance to a group has a strong positive correlation with the difficulty in belonging to the group. The more you have to give up in order to belong to a group, the more highly you prize your membership in the group.

In general, the more rigorous a belief system is, the more adamant its adherents are that their faith is correct.

Most members of the religious faith community would probably argue that the fact that their belief system has withstood the test of time is strong evidence for its authenticity. On the contrary, I think it is strong evidence for how we tend to believe incredible things which we are taught as children and that others around us believe, for the difficulty we have accepting our own mortality, for our need to belong, and for our need to be right.

As Mark Twain noted, only partly exaggerating, "faith is believing what you know ain't so."

THE BORN AGAIN SYNDROME

If religion -- or let's make it specific for this discussion -- if Christianity is not what it claims to be, how can you explain the phenomenon of the change that takes place in converts, some converts anyway, when they see the light and "give their hearts to Jesus?"

Let me be the first to admit that there are many instances of profound change occurring when people have had a genuine religious conversion experience. Scoundrels have become saints (to use the term most often ascribed to such people -- although in reality, there is no such thing as a saint), cheaters have become trustworthy, liars have become honest, brutal villains have become pillars of society.

How can this not be real? Oh, it's real enough, all right. And when it is genuine, it can be a life-changing event. The Christian community refers to it as being "born again", and it sometimes seems almost as dramatic as if a totally new person were inhabiting the old, familiar body.

The term "born again" comes primarily from one

story in the New Testament, told only in the last of the four gospels to be written. (I mention this only because it likely means that the term itself was not common among early Christians, certainly not among those who were attracted to Jesus during his lifetime.) The story in John 3 is about a high muckety-muck in the Jewish faith, a man named Nicodemus, who came to talk to Jesus after dark because he didn't want his buddies to know. He is pictured as being a genuine seeker who recognized that Jesus must be something special. Jesus tells him that it isn't enough to be showing passing interest, that in order to "see the kingdom of God" a person has to be born again. Jesus goes on to answer Nicodemus' perplexity by explaining that he is referring to being born of the spirit. He even counters apparent skepticism by using the analogy that you can't see the wind, but you can feel its effects.

This story is followed by perhaps the most familiar passage in the entire Christian bible, John 3:16. Even if you're not religious, you're probably familiar with this bible verse. You've likely seen hand-lettered signs being lofted at a ball game or other gathering with this Biblical reference. It simply says that God loved the world so much that he was willing to let his own son be killed so that people's sins could be forgiven. If you ignore the logical question about why this all-powerful God decided to make up the rule that something living had to be killed before he could bring himself to stop blaming folks for messing up, it's a sweet sentiment. At least the "loving-the-world" part has sort of a friendly ring. In any event, this is the Biblical basis for the notion that in order to be a true believer, you have to be born again.

So if some folks follow this formula and become

really, really different people, why be skeptical? Maybe being born again is just what it claims to be.

Well, maybe, but there are at least two big problems with accepting this carte blanche.

The first is what I call The True Believer phenomenon. Simply put, it means that whenever a person is truly convinced that a given experience or ritual or ceremony is going to make a significant change in his life, chances are pretty good that it will. I don't know what the odds are, maybe not even as much as fifty/fifty, but it still happens enough to catch our attention. Sometimes the change is dramatic. Sometimes it's much less so, with the difference being explained by any number of factors, which I'll address in a bit.

But the important thing to note is that such life-changing experiences happen in all kinds of settings and in response to all kinds of belief systems, some religious, some not. Virtually all religions are filled with people who claim that they became different people when they converted to their faith. They may or may not use the term "born again", but they certainly describe what happened to them in ways indistinguishable from the stories of "born again" church folks, and their subsequent living patterns support their claims. Such people explain the transformation in whatever terms are used by the system they've embraced. And they generally are convinced that their belief system has unveiled a truth that people in other systems have missed. Often they think that their own brand of faith is the only one in the world that can produce such miraculous transformations.

The reality is that lots of non-religious experiences

produce life-changing conversions, also. Change of political party affiliation has been known to produce huge changes in people, especially if politics was already an important part of their lives. Membership in a self-help or therapy group has often changed participants' lives in profound ways. In earlier days in this country membership in the Masonic Order, with its secret symbols and signs, was sometimes the defining influence in a person's life. And certainly becoming a fellow traveler, as in the communist party, has changed many a person to someone his/her former friends wouldn't recognize.

I'm not suggesting that all conversion experiences that dramatically change people have equally sanguine results. Let's look at the Heaven's Gate group again, for example. Here was a group of people who imbibed in a particular belief system that most people would describe as bizarre. It led many of the men to castrate themselves. It led all of the members of this group to totally cut themselves off from family and other friends and devote all their waking hours to living out their commitment. In the end, they ended their own lives in a mass suicide, apparently without any forceful coercion other than the strength of their leader's ideas. No one could deny that these people had undergone dramatic, and tragic, transformation. Any objective observer would have to admit that this qualifies as a "born again" experience. They became different people. Their whole lives changed. Never mind that those of us on the outside of this belief system don't view the changes as positive. The changes still happened.

Why? Because of the power of some god? I hardly think so. A much more likely explanation is that they had reasons to want a transforming change to take place, they were told it would happen, and their very expectation helped bring it about, especially since they lived full-time with others who thought the same way.

It happens all the time, in all kinds of settings, some with more positive results than others. Being "born again" is not restricted to any particular belief system, which means that it isn't the truth of any one belief system that makes such transformations occur. It is how powerfully the person believes it will happen and how motivated he/she is to see that it does. In other contexts this is called the "placebo effect". Every careful researcher in medicine, psychology, and many other disciplines knows the power of this effect. If you believe something you've taken or done or said will make a difference, good chance that it will. There are other psychological factors involved, also, but the possible combinations are so numerous that we'd get bogged down trying to spell them all out. Instead, let me give you a real-life example of a secular born-again experience.

When I was in the early stage of my career as a psychologist, a new system of psychotherapy burst on the scene. It was called Neuro-Linguistic Programming, NLP in the jargon of the day. It was started by a couple of young honchos in California who put on an impressive show and who were able to convince lots of therapist types who attended their workshops that this system was tapping into heretofore hidden aspects of human behavior and would enable skilled practitioners to become much more powerful change agents. Their ideas had some intriguing aspects, and even though there was very little well-designed research to support their claims, some of their therapeutic methods seemed to have merit, and I was able to incorporate some of them into my own practice.

However, I did not become a true believer, a groupie within this movement. But some of my colleagues who attended the introductory workshop with me, and who were also at an early stage in their careers, did. They attended advanced workshops, read everything being written about this theoretical framework, adopted a whole new language for describing their therapeutic interventions, wanted to talk about nothing else, and gave every evidence that NLP had taken over and transformed their lives. It was a "born again" experience in every way -- except that it was entirely secular!

I'm not knocking NLP as a therapeutic approach or suggesting that it doesn't have merit. Many a client who went to these therapists after they became certified NLP practitioners also experienced significant life changes, particularly if s/he moved in similar social circles and began to adopt the language peculiar to this movement. I am only saying that I was a close-up witness to a secular conversion phenomenon that had all the earmarks of what the evangelical religious community call being "born again." But it had absolutely no religious or theological foundation whatsoever.

Why did I not also become a true believer? Who knows? Maybe it was because I was a bit older than some of my friends who were at a similar stage in their careers as therapists. Or maybe it was because I had seen lots of the "snake oil salesmen" type of ministers in my earlier career, and my antennae were attuned to pick up any signals that this might not be all that was being claimed. Maybe it was because the system demanded too much suspension of rational analysis and reminded me of what I had been through in the ministry. I don't know for sure, and it isn't really important anyway.

What is important is to point out that "born again" experiences happen in lots of settings, and the primary reason for their efficacy seems to depend upon the person's believing, "feeling", that they have somehow been changed.

Sometimes the change is permanent. Sometimes not. If the convert is a part of an on-going group (a church congregation in the religious tradition), it increases the likelihood that the change will be lasting. But it doesn't guarantee it.

Which leads me to the second problem with accepting the "born again" idea carte blanch -- it fails to work a whole lot of the time. What do I mean? Well, I mean simply that following the formula is no guarantee you'll get the predicted results. For every instance in which being "born again" leads to a dramatic change that is discernible to others, there are easily as many instances in which there is no observable change at all.

Why? Well, true believers would say that the person simply wasn't sincere in her/his conversion experience. I'm sure there are many cases in which that is true. But that cannot be the main reason. I know personally scores of people who are absolutely convinced they did everything right in trying to get the "born again" experience to occur, who were as sincere as they could be, and nothing happened.

I propose that there are three factors involved in whether the "born again" experience is a real and powerful one for people who give it a go: (1) how desperate the person is for a change; (2) how much emotion is engendered in the experience; and (3) how much regular contact they have with others who believe the way they do. Let's look briefly at each.

(1) The more dramatic the need for a change, the more powerful the born-again experience. Simply put, this means that if a person is really down and out, has hit rock bottom in some way and is desperately looking for something to make his life better, you have the setting for a lollapalooza of a conversion experience.

Someone who has experienced frightening trauma like a life-threatening accident or frightening medical diagnosis, someone who has come to the end of the road with substance abuse, someone whose financial security has been devastated, someone who has experienced the grief of death, dismemberment, divorce -- this kind of "end of my rope" experience provides powerful incentive for people to latch on to something that promises a new beginning.

(2) The more powerful the emotion a person feels in the conversion experience, the more likely it is to make a lasting impression. All conversion advocates bank on this phenomenon, and most often an attempt is made to heighten any emotion that is present. Bowing your head, kneeling or prostrating yourself, closing your eyes -- all these and many more standard conversion postures encourage an upwelling of emotion.

It is no accident that emotion-laden music is used during altar calls. The part that music has played in keeping religion going throughout the centuries could hardly be overemphasized, and nowhere is this more evident than in the situation in which potential converts are being challenged to give up old ways and become "born again." In the evangelical Christian tradition they are called "invitation hymns," and every attempt is made to play on people's emotions, both from the wording used and the plaintive nature of the music.

In the Southern Baptist church to which I gave the first half of my life, the favorite invitation hymn began with these words:

Just as I am without one plea
But that Thy blood was shed for me
And that Thou bidst me come to Thee;
O Lamb of God, I come, I come.

If you are feeling as if your life is in shambles, if you've been promised that a simple act of asserting your faith will turn everything around, and if you are surrounded by the plaintive words and notes of this hymn, easy to see how you might suspend all other reality and take the plunge. And that the experience would be remembered as so powerful that something mystical, but real, must have taken place.

(3) The third element, being surrounded by other believers who welcome you into the group and who reinforce your new belief system, is the clincher. The power of group approval, acceptance, and support cannot possibly be overemphasized. We are social animals. And I think it is manifestly evident that the need for social contact, for belonging to a group, is a part of the genetic inheritance of humans as a species.

Most of the vertebrates are also social animals, and essentially all the higher primates are. Although evolution has given humans the capacity to evaluate rationally the influence of the group on our perceptions, the power of the need to belong often overwhelms trust in our own rational processes, a fact not lost on religious or other convert-seeking groups.

When these three factors are present in a conversion experience, the likelihood of a significant change occurring is increased. When any one of them is missing or weak, the likelihood of a powerful change is diminished. My observation is that the effect is more multiplicative than additive, which just means that if each one could be measured on a 1 to 10 scale, the final effect wouldn't be just whatever the numbers yielded if added together, but rather whatever the product was if the numbers were multiplied against each other. So, the strong presence of all three makes for a very strong effect indeed.

Let me use as an example a prominent member of the Watergate scandal who became "born again" in the Christian faith while in prison, Charles Colson. Since he is a public figure, most people are probably familiar with his story. He has become a powerful example of someone whose life was really transformed and whose life following this experience has been dramatically different. As an outside observer, I would say that all three of the necessary elements were present in his situation. According to what I read, he is totally dedicated to helping others whose lives have run aground and is quite successful in helping scores of prisoners.

But this kind of change doesn't always happen. And even when it does, it doesn't always last. It is not, as religion claims, that God reaches down and transforms a person who has followed the formula for "salvation", and this person is forevermore a different person. Anyone who has been a part of any religious organization, and who is honest, would have to admit that church members come in all kinds, just as unchurched people do. Some of them appear to be filled with the milk of human kindness. Many of them do not.

I fervently wish the simple formula for becoming a new and different and transformed person were really accurate and that the shining examples of people for whom the conversion experience has worked were really a product of divine intervention and transformation. I wish the evidence supported that claim.

It simply doesn't.

BLOODY RELIGION: A BLOODY SHAME

Blood is front and center in the three Abrahamic religions – Judaism, Christianity, and Islam. You can talk all you want about the core of religion being love and grace, but you can't get there in these three orthodox religions without wading through an ocean of blood.

The basic concept is simple, to wit: without the shedding of blood there is no remission of sins. That's incredibly simple. It's also incredible: that is, unbelievable for anyone with a modicum of logical sense who actually takes the time to analyse it.

Why is it incredible?

Well, think about it. Pretend you've never heard it before. Here's an all-powerful God who creates a world and populates it with various forms of life. He allows the crown of his creation, human beings, to disobey in such a way that he can't just let it go. He has to either punish them or figure out some sort of ritual they can perform so he can forgive them. So he decides that the ritual will be this: take an innocent animal (who's not able to disobey the rules and thus displease this God, by the way, and who, interestingly enough, is always a non-predator in the animal kingdom) and slit its throat. Let its blood pour out on the ground while it dies. Then this all-powerful God can smile and say, "Okay, I forgive your screwing up this time, but don't let it happen again or you'll have to kill another innocent, peaceable animal to appease me."

Again I ask that you think about this as if you had never heard it before. Given that this God could have made it any way he chose, does it make any kind of sense whatsoever that this would have been his brilliant solution to the problem of human beings screwing up?

I don't know if you've ever thought about how horrendous the story of Abraham being told to sacrifice his son Isaac is, but I dare you to really consider what a terrible message this gives. God supposedly told Abraham that he should take his son to a special mountain and kill and burn him in order to prove that he loved God. According to the story in Genesis 22, the father even had his trusting son carry the wood for the fire and answered the boy's question about where the animal was that would be killed and burned without telling him what he had in mind to do. Once there, he bound his son, laid him on the wood and was ready to kill him before this loving God decided Abraham had proved his faith and intervened to save the boy.

O happy day!

Can you imagine what that did for the boy's trust in his father? Suppose this were a modern story about some father in your community. The boy lives to tell the tale, which he does to the authorities. Wouldn't you think this man was an utter lunatic if he explained that God had told him to do it? Of course you would, and you'd be right. And this lunatic father who claimed he heard his God telling him to kill and burn his son would be treated for the mental illness he was exhibiting.

But times were different then? Yeah, right. Try telling that to the boy whose father was ready to kill and burn him in order to show how much he loved God.

Wouldn't you think a humane God would have realized this wasn't such a swell way to test someone's faithfulness, that it would scar the boy for life and send a horrible message about what it takes to please this almighty being? How in the name of all that is precious can anybody justify the idea that the only way to be able to forgive somebody who has done something bad is to kill some innocent living being!

"Without the shedding of blood, there is no remission of sin" -- what a sick idea!

Let me try again to put it in modern terms. Suppose you have a daughter who disobeys you. Let's say she slips out of the house to be with her boyfriend and lies to you about it. You find out what happened and say to her, "Before I can forgive you, you have to kill something -- your little pet Yorkie who sleeps in your bed every night." So your daughter takes her beloved pet, slits its throat with a butcher knife while tears roll down her cheeks, lets it bleed to death as the little pet looks up at her with incredulous eyes, and then you say, "Okay, now I forgive you."

Would you be a monster or what! It's incomprehensible, isn't it? Nobody in his right mind would do such a thing. But that's what we're told this brilliant, loving, all-powerful God decided was the way it should be. Throughout the entire Bible there is never any questioning of the barbarity of this scheme.

And it gets worse, of course. When Jesus is executed in a horrible way (according to accepted religious mythology), it is interpreted that his death was the final and ultimate sacrifice, the quintessential spilling of blood that would allow God to forgive all sins thereafter by harking back to this particular gory spectacle. So there are countless references in church hymnody to the power of the blood. We're supposed to immerse ourselves in it, wash our clothes in it, glory in it, and rejoice in it -- ad nauseam. This is blood we're talking about.

Blood!

Somehow God has decided that killing some innocent being, which is also supposed to be God's creation by the way, is the best and only way to show devotion to an almighty being. Is there any way to make that idea make sense?

The most sacred ritual of the church throughout the centuries has been built around the notion of symbolically drinking Jesus' blood. In the Roman Catholic tradition, the claim is made that the wine of the Eucharist actually becomes Jesus' blood. Most protestant groups reject this idea as being a bit much, but nonetheless blithely go ahead with the idea that symbolically drinking Jesus' blood is honoring him.

When we hear about a primitive tribe that vanquishes a foe and ritualistically eats the still beating heart that has been ripped from the slain enemy's breast and drinks a goblet of the still warm blood, we are repulsed. As well we should be. Why, oh why, then, are we not able to look realistically at the equally repulsive notion that the God of this universe required that innocent, living beings had to be ritualistically killed, with their blood oozing out onto the ground, in order for him to forgive us for being human and screwing up?

Any way you look at it, this is a bloody religion.

And I say it's a bloody shame!

IN RELIGION, SIN IS SPELLED S-E-X

I can't be sure at this point in my life, but I think that my first genuine feeling of having committed what the church calls sin occurred at puberty. By that time I had been a baptized church member for several years, but the only bad behaviors I was aware of were things like talking during church service or refusing to eat liver unless I was forced to. Those were things I hoped wouldn't be noticed and punished, but they weren't accompanied by internal angst. I had no feeling of having done something bad or "sinned" as religion puts it.

Then puberty hit, and sexual interest became the most powerful force in my world. Since there was no accurate information available either at school or in our family, mistaken notions predominated, and curiosity coupled with hormonal drive started to intrude mightily on my internal sense of being a good person.

In short, I now felt horribly sinful!

I don't mean that I intellectually thought that perhaps I was somewhat sinful. I mean I felt totally depraved, awful, dirty, unworthy, completely and absolutely sinful. And since, once I had discovered masturbation, no amount of resolve to never do it again would last more than a few days or weeks, I was regularly reminded just how perverse, and probably unredeemable, I must be.

Why? Because the faith of my fathers had set it up for this to happen. Although enlightened church members, like many of my friends and family, would never make the mistake of teaching their children to equate sex with sin in the manner of my family of origin, there is still the underlying message throughout most religions (certainly all western religions) that sin and sex are handmaidens.

Let's take a look at the message that the supposed guidebook of the Judeo-Christian faith, the Bible, gives on the subject. We'll hit only the highlights because an exhaustive look would be . . well, exhausting.

The Garden of Eden story (which any true Biblical scholar knows is pure myth, not history) starts with the assumption that the first couple was innocent and sinless to begin with. It makes a point of saying that Adam and Eve were both naked and were not ashamed. I assume that the intended implication is that they hadn't noticed differences in anatomy between male and female. I don't know how long that innocent condition was supposed to have lasted, but I can tell you this for sure: if hormones were present and they were walking around naked, it couldn't have lasted very blooming long!

Anyhow, the story talks about how there was one tree in this idyllic setting that they were not to bother, called the tree of the knowledge of good and evil. And in true male chauvinistic tradition that continues to this day, the story has the female being enticed by the wily snake (phallic symbol, anyone?) to disobey the rules and to seduce the innocent male to join her in eating forbidden fruit. Voila! Suddenly they are aware that they are naked and make some fig-leaf improvisations to cover the genital portion of that condition. Then God swoops down with almighty anger and makes them fess up, whereupon they are overwhelmed with shame. Adam blames Eve, of course, and even blames God tangentially by reminding him that this mistake was caused by the "woman that YOU gave me." But God is having none of it, banishes them from the now soiled garden and (make note of this carefully) tells the woman that for her punishment she will have to bear children with great pain. The story ends with God himself making them clothes of skins so they wouldn't have to walk around naked. Horrors! Nakedness, no less. Oh my, my, my!

Although the story is myth, not history, the message couldn't be clearer: the forbidden tree was sex. Engaging in sex was what enlightened them about good and evil. Sex was what made them aware and ashamed of their nakedness. Sex was the "original sin" that tainted all humankind down through the ages even unto this very day.

That's the Biblical story, and it's utter and absolute balderdash! Given that all living things, including many plants, rely on the exchange between the two sexes to reproduce, and given that in the creation story/myth God instituted this way of spreading living things around the world, why should reproduction have been different for the first human couple? The animals over which they were supposed to rule obviously copulated to reproduce offspring, and the process of childbirth for the female animal was surely accompanied with considerable pain. Adam and Eve were equipped to use this same method to bear young, this equipment having been supplied by the creator, including, one presumes, the hormonal desire to engage in intimate sexual behavior. What possible sense does it make to imply that sexual intercourse was breaking the rules and that henceforth childbirth for the human female would be accompanied by pain?

Answer: it makes zero sense. But it explains the religious teaching that all human beings are born tainted by sin because all of them are born via sexual intimacy. (As an aside, artificial insemination and/or in vitro fertilization both bypass the usual method of inserting semen into a uterus. Thus, the "sin" of sexual intercourse is not involved in this kind of procreation. But I guess traditional religionists would say that the damage was already done eons ago, and there's no escaping original sin no matter how you are able to get pregnant. Just one of many incongruities religion conveniently ignores.)

One more mythical story from the pre-history part of the first Bible book, Genesis, has to do with what happened with Noah after the flood. He got drunk and was lying in his tent naked when one of his three sons, Ham, walked in and saw him. The Bible makes it a point to say that Ham "looked upon his father's nakedness." He informs his two brothers who walk backwards into the tent to cover up their father, being extra careful not to catch a glimpse of pop in the buff. But when Noah awakes he somehow knows that Ham has beheld him in an unclothed state and curses, get this, not Ham, but Ham's son Canaan. He formally declares that Canaan and his descendants are destined to be slaves to the descendants of his uncles, Shem and

Japheth.   Here you have an irony of ironies.   For something no worse than happening to see his father's sexual organs while Noah is sleeping off a drunk, the son of the offender and all his lineage is cursed to the horrors of slavery down through the ages.   Can you imagine that slavery, one of the most atrocious insults to human decency in all of history, is presented as having been due to a minor event involving nakedness? This mythical story only underscores the fact that from its earliest inception, religion has presented sex as a shameful, sinful thing.   Other sins, like murder for instance, don't hold a candle to sex for religionists in the hierarchy of big, bad sins.

Throughout the rest of the thirty-nine books that make up the Hebrew Bible (Christians refer to it as the Old Testament), sin is referred to in sexual terms. The favorite one is "whore." Whenever God is upset with some of his chosen brood, he has his prophets accuse them of "whoring after other gods", or some similar sexual epithet.

Then there is the unquestioned command to cut off the penile foreskin of all the male descendants of Abraham in order to show membership in God's chosen group. Circumcision became the norm, and although it is unclear how this made sex any less offensive to the Almighty, it is quite clear that this unnecessary procedure had to do with sex, not with urination, the penis' other regular function. God-followers are even enjoined to be sure their hearts are circumcised so as not to displease God. Though this is clearly meant in a figurative sense, it points up the pervasiveness of sexual imagery in referring to sinful behavior.

But let's go now to the piece de resistance of religion's equating of sex with sin -- the idea of the virgin birth of Jesus. There are myriad explanations given by genuine Biblical scholars about how this story got started and how the word translated "virgin" in Isaiah's prophecy about a messiah really simply meant "a young woman of marriageable age." But I'm not concerned here with sorting through any of those issues. What I am anxious to point out is that religion assumes that if you were going to have a perfect (read that sinless) person sent to be the savior, he would have to be conceived in some way other than sexual intercourse. Why?

Because in religion, sex equals sin!

The whole idea of the virgin birth is, of course, to make Jesus out to be bigger than life, a superhuman person (which is discussed in the chapter about Jesus as Paul Bunyan). But the fact that a primary way of presenting this purity of Jesus is to say that no sex was involved in his conception is to point up how sinlessness means having no connection whatever with sex. In the Roman Catholic tradition, it was even decided centuries later Mary, the mother of Jesus, must have received a special dispensation when she was born, so that even though she was conceived by normal sexual intercourse between her parents, Mary was born "sinless", unlike other regular people. This was so that she could be the holy (sinless) vessel for the virgin birth of Jesus. This is referred to as the "immaculate conception". There is no other reason for this story to have arisen except that religion (the Judeo-Christian version) equates sex with sin.

Of course, traditional religionists of a fundamentalist persuasion would argue that the reason the virgin birth was necessary was that Jesus was to be divine, not simply human. And they would, of course, argue that it really happened that way. But anyone who would believe that a literal virgin birth occurred, and that this fact is terribly important, would also believe that a literal flood covered the whole world in Noah's day with a pair of each animal being saved in a literal boat, that a literal burning bush spoke to a guy named Moses, and that a God who made this universe picked out one bunch of people to be his favorites, with the rest of the world's peoples not counting for diddly. On and on goes the list of ridiculous assumptions that a literal reading of the Bible demands. I won't even begin to try to convince people who still hold to such untenable ideas that none of this is factually accurate.

What I do wish to do, however, is help people who have already acknowledged how unbelievable such literal reading of the Bible is to see that the whole concept of sin that needs forgiving is based upon the mistaken notion that human sexuality results from sinfulness, is an expression of our sinful nature, and that refraining from sex enables a person to achieve a higher righteousness. This leads us to the role celibacy has played in the Christian church through the ages.

The idea of a celibate priesthood, with its later concomitant celibate nunhood, probably got its start from the letters of Paul in the New Testament part of the Christian Bible, primarily in 1 Corinthians 7. The chapter begins with the consummately ridiculous assertion that it would be better for a man never to touch a woman. Just think for a moment about how utterly silly that notion is. If the whole world had followed that advice, obviously we wouldn't be around to be discussing it today since humankind would have become extinct within a few decades. He goes on to talk about the allowable concession to human weakness that manages to allow sex without offending the Almighty, namely marriage. But he makes it a point to say that it would be much more pleasing to God if everybody were unmarried as, it is assumed, was Paul himself and thus, supposedly, totally refrained from sex. Although the writer (Paul) of this letter says several times that he's not sure he has a direct line to God on this issue, that caveat was conveniently ignored as the church began to gain power and influence. Before you knew it, the ethos evolved that for those who wanted to achieve a higher righteousness, celibacy was the only way to go. And for centuries the established church followed the policy of insisting that all its chosen and ordained leaders (priests, nuns, monks, friars) had to renounce sex and live as asexual beings.

It didn't work out very well, of course, because for most people, living with no sexual outlet is pretty doggoned tough. The Pauline assertion that having regular sex causes a person to focus more on worldly things is one hundred and eighty degrees off. NOT having sex leads to sexual thoughts dominating one's every waking moment for a whole bunch of folks. Having no sexual outlet doesn't make the drive disappear, and few things distract a person from responsibilities more than being horny all the time. So multitudinous stories about clandestine sexual activity among the supposedly celibate church leadership are rife. No need to try to determine what percentage of those stories is factually accurate. The reality is that if a person has a normal sex drive, trying to deny it is terribly frustrating and often futile. And the idea that doing so is a more righteous, holy kind of life and is more pleasing to God -- well, it's just too, too absurd for words.

One other problem that this ridiculous notion gave rise to is the fact that people with a homosexual orientation often chose religious vocation. Two obvious reasons come to mind. One is that until quite recent times gays had a tough time feeling okay about themselves, and going into the priesthood just might help atone (in their minds) for feeling decidedly unworthy. Some probably even hoped that the more holy state of the priesthood just might make them no longer have homosexual thoughts and urges. The other is that it gave them a convenient excuse for not wanting to marry. But this made subsequent inability to keep vows of chastity even more problematic. When a priest seduces trusting altar boys, it causes serious upheaval among the faithful. But the system that insists on a celibate priesthood is a setup for this kind of lamentable abuse to occur.

I don't want to leave the impression that homosexual orientation is in any way synonymous with pedophilia. It isn't, of course, though religious conservatives often imply that the two go hand in hand. Pedophilia involves serious psychopathology which needs treatment. Homosexuality is a variant of sexual identity which appears to occur naturally in most, if not all, of the vertebrate animal population.

The protestant revolt against the established church included rejecting the idea of a celibate ministry. The Roman church would probably like to change their position on this issue these days, too, but they could hardly do so without losing face big time. Having insisted through all these centuries that celibacy is more pleasing to God than connubiality, relaxing the rules now would cost them hugely in popular support among their adherents. The idea of religious vocation as sacrament, which Roman Catholic families hold, is strongly dependent on the notion that celibacy is a higher righteousness. The RC hierarchy is not about to concede that this is nonsense and that they have been wrong all these centuries. The uproar would be deafening. Better to try to do damage control when stories emerge, as increasingly they are these days, about their clergy having strayed from the straight and narrow and treat such instances as aberrations, rather than being quite predictable from the misguided notion that celibacy is a desirable lifestyle.

Another unfortunate notion that affects the entire membership of the Roman Catholic Church is that sexual activity must never be enjoyed for its own sake. Only procreative sex is sanctioned. This is why any birth control method other than the rhythm method or sexual abstinence is officially forbidden in this version of Christianity. Who knows how many otherwise loyal Catholics choose to ignore this silly and problematic proscription! As well they should, since very large families are increasingly difficult to feed, clothe and educate in today's complex society.

It is clear that the reason for the religious stance that all allowable sex must have procreation as a possible result is that sexual activity that is enjoyed for its own sake is somehow displeasing to God. Why else would masturbation be considered wrong? Or sex between consenting unmarried adults? Or adult-choice prostitution? Or homosexual relationships? There is no other explanation for all these prohibitions about sex that religion has insisted on other than the basic belief that sexual pleasure is sinful, offends the

Almighty and needs to be tightly controlled even when it is allowed as a concession to our human weakness.

Like any other powerful force, sex can be misused and abused, so I'm not suggesting that ethical standards of conduct can be abandoned. What I am saying is that religion has been decidedly behind the curve in its understanding of the role sex plays in human society. The reason? A fundamental mistaken assertion that sex is anti-spiritual.

In recent years some of the more enlightened religious groups have been willing to make attempts at remedying this unfortunate situation. Some churches are now ordaining clergy who are openly homosexual and are giving church sanction to gay relationships. There are a few wonderful sex education programs for youth in some churches that attempt to undo the damage that has been done by the majority religious teaching on sex down through the years. In order to do so, these church groups have to acknowledge that the Hebrew/Christian Bible is sadly misleading on the subject, as indeed it is on many things.

I haven't addressed the issue of whether the concept of sin itself is tenable. The answer is straight-forward. No, it isn't. Not in its most widely-accepted definition, which is that sin is a violation of religious law as it represents the law of God. The reality is that we don't have any law of God. Not in the Bible. Not anywhere else. We have moral and ethical standards which have evolved throughout human history, but religion's take on those standards is usually unduly restrictive and based on the superstitious notion that somebody was able to access the revelation of an almighty being. This simply hasn't happened.

It might be easier for traditional believers to

acknowledge this assumption if they thought about how convinced followers of other religions are that they also have received instruction from on high. The Muslin fundamentalists are a good case in point. They are so convinced of the truth of their "revelation" that they are often willing to martyr themselves to advance their belief system. And they have instituted "reforms" in the name of religion when they have taken over their government institutions, as in Iran and Afghanistan, which have perpetrated horrible injustices against the population, particularly the section of the population which is female.

Nowhere is this clearer than on the issue that sin and sex are intertwined. The plight of women in these fundamentalist Islamic countries is a direct result of the idea that sexual interest is prohibited except within very narrow limits. The terrible abuses that have been heaped on women simply for being women are almost unbelievable. Even granting that the male chauvinistic insistence on power is also a part of this pitiful situation, why would religious leadership want to punish women so shamefully? Because of the same mistaken notion that the Hebrew/Christian Bible espouses, namely that the essence of sin as rebellion against the laws of God is sex.

Because sex is such a ubiquitous drive, this fundamental error in accepted religious doctrine is not just a minor matter.

The idea that sin is spelled S-E-X. That's a major screw up.

UNTOUCHED BY AN ANGEL

Wouldn't it be nice if each of us really did have a guardian angel whose only job was to look out for us and make sure nothing bad happened to us? How uncommonly comforting it would be to know that an unseen, but powerful and benevolent being was taking every step with us, making sure we didn't make a wrong turn. Or fall down. Or even twist an ankle!

Would everyone who has ever actually seen an angel (everyone who is not certifiably mentally ill, that is) please raise your hand?

What, no hands raised?

How can that be when there is so much belief in their existence? Could it be that just as in simpler times, when magical thinking was the norm, people believed in elves and leprechauns, without ever having seen one, because it was socially acceptable to do so, people continue to believe in angels in these relatively sophisticated days because it is chic to do so?

Must be something like that, because otherwise we'd have to conclude that mental illness is much more widespread than we assumed. The latest figures I came across suggested that over 60% of the populace in this country believe in the existence of angels. In other words, more than half the otherwise-intelligent people you meet answer "yes" to the question, "Do you believe in angels?" even though nobody (as in not anybody at all, none, zero, zilch) has ever seen an angel.

One of the more popular recent TV programs is about a group of angels who intervene in human affairs on an ad hoc basis. It is called, appropriately enough for the fantasy it depicts, Touched By An Angel. I was never able to suspend logical thought processes long enough to watch an episode all the way through, but it apparently had enough gooey factor to have a large stable of regular viewers. There is a lot of make-believe in TV programs, but grown-ups are usually able to tell the difference between fantasy as entertainment and the real world. The Star Trek series, for example, had multiplied thousands of devotees, some of them quite intelligent, who attended Trekkie conventions and collected Trekkie memorabilia, but they didn't begin to think that it was anything but fantasy.

Apparently where the fantasy involves religious belief, the same rules don't apply.

Since 100% of intelligent adults stop believing in Santa Claus and the Easter Bunny once they leave young childhood, why do so many otherwise mature adults continue to believe in angels or, for that matter, in devils, which also do not exist?

One possible explanation is that both angels and devils (or demons) are mentioned in "sacred" religious literature. If someone takes the position that every word in the Bible is factually accurate, it follows that this same person, who has never seen an angel or a devil, would continue to believe these beings exist. But this can't be the entire explanation since not even close to 60% of the population of this country believes that every word in the Christian Bible is factually true, including most people who still cling to the notion that the Bible is the inspired "Word of God." Most educated people know that the Bible contains monumental historical inaccuracies and incongruities.

Besides, if Biblical depictions of angels were the primary reason a majority of the population professes to believe in these non-existent beings, our ideas about what they are like would be quite different. Angels in Biblical story come in all kinds, some presented as gentle and benign such as in the story about how the angel Gabriel appeared to Mary to whisper that she was most blessed among women in that she was going to get pregnant without sex (a novel concept for many reasons which are discussed in the previous chapter) and seemed to cause no consternation or fear.

Others are depicted as contentious or ferocious, like the one who wrestled with Jacob all night. Or like the one God sent to destroy 70,000 Israelites because King David had the audacity to order a census of his subjects, which inexplicably upset God something fierce. In case you're not familiar with this story (told in 1st Chronicles 20-21 of the Christian Bible), let me recount it briefly for you.

The story begins by telling how King David's armies defeated a bunch of the other folks who lived in that part of the world. Some of them sound like fairly interesting specimens, with six fingers on each hand and six toes on each foot, but obviously God didn't give a flip about them because he regularly ordered their slaughter, including pregnant women having their bellies ripped open and children having their heads dashed against stones. Once victory was complete and

God had been praised, David plundered all the valuables he could handle and set the people he let live to working as slaves.

None of this bothered God, according to the Biblical story, because God was helping David out in his battles to begin with, God needing to slaughter indigenous peoples in order to prove he was the most powerful God around, you know. But then David took a notion to find out just how many people his kingdom now included and ordered a census. And that, dear friends, is what ticked God off.

Don't ask me why. Who can understand the "ways of God"? The census was taken and revealed over a million and a half men, with women and children obviously not being worth counting since they didn't carry swords. Well, whatever it was about this census that riled God so, He wasn't going to take it lying down and sent word to King David that punishment was on the way and he could choose his poison: (1) three years of famine; (2) three months of utter devastation by his enemies (I guess God was going to help out the bad guys this time -- that's how ticked off he was!); or (3) three days of pestilence throughout the land wielded by an angel with the sword of the Lord.

Talk about a tough choice! Three sets of "threes", and none of them targeting the one who had issued the dastardly census order, which even David himself pointed out to God. But God was too bummed to listen to any mealy-mouthed pleading and told David he'd best decide which of the three choices he wanted in a hurry because God was getting madder by the minute.

Well, David decided he'd rather get it over with ASAP and opted for the angel with the sword. Within three days, 70,000 of God's obedient servants, who had done nothing except allow themselves to be counted in the census, were killed. The angel was having a grand ol' time of it and was heading toward Jerusalem with his sword raised when God decided maybe He had done enough for now. The angel was disappointed big time, because he was really getting good at this slaughtering business. If you're an angel who can't be seen except by certain people, and you have a sword of pestilence with which to do God's bidding, you can mess up a whole lot of folks real fast. Since everybody likes to be good at what he/she does and since this angel was rapidly becoming a world-class destroyer, one of the Almighty's best, you can see why he was kinda let down. But after David made a special deal with a local farmer to buy his threshing barn so that he could burn it up with all kinds of appeasement offerings to God, God told the angel to put his sword back in his sheath. And the game was over. For now.

Lovely story, eh what! Anyway, the point is that angels in religious literature are not all loving, benevolent beings. And the persistent notion that everybody has a guardian angel who looks out for them must come from something other than a literal reading of religious scripture.

So why should a majority of the population in the USA profess to believe that these creatures, which no one has ever seen, are nonetheless real? My best guess is that the explanation lies in the pernicious human desire to not have to be responsible.

Before you dismiss this as a possible explanation, consider how much energy we expend trying to be sure we don't get blamed for stuff. The comedian Flip Wilson's portrayal of Geraldine is best remembered for her line, "The devil made me do it!" In other words, I'm not responsible, so don't blame me.

One of the first responses children learn to make when something or somebody has made a mess is, "I didn't do it. It's not my fault." When punishment for messes is the norm, the don't-blame-me response becomes almost knee-jerk.

A few years ago on a vacation trip a detour took us through the little community of Joyce, Washington, which consisted of a school, a ball field, and a general store -- and not much else. Inside the store we discovered that this community had decided to make book of the fact that it was small and unknown by selling things with "I LOVE JOYCE" on them as if it were a well-known place. Since my wife is named Joyce, we bought t-shirts and buttons, and we also bought a mock diploma from the (non-existent) University of Joyce, the motto for which was "mea culpa non", which the certificate explained meant "It's a notta my fault."

All kidding aside, I'm convinced that lots of people would be happy to have as their assigned tag line, "Don't blame me. It's not my fault." Think of all the bumper stickers that proclaim, "Don't blame me, I voted for _____ (insert name of elected official of choice.) These stickers wouldn't be humorous and sell briskly if it weren't for the ubiquity of the desire to not have to be responsible.

I guess it's understandable. Human beings are faced daily with so many uncertainties, many of them including personal decisions. How can you ever know for sure that you are making the best choice? You can't. As Lincoln observed, life has to be lived forwards, but it can only be understood backwards. The passage of time lets us know whether we've made good choices or not. I'm not talking only about those times when we know what the right thing is but choose not to do it because the wrong thing is more appealing. I mean the far more numerous times when it isn't at all clear what the best choice is, but we have to choose anyhow.

I'm convinced that most decisions we make must be made on the basis of insufficient data and that all life's important decisions have to be made in the face of tons of unknowable data. If you can get enough information in advance to know for sure what the best course of action is, it is likely a relatively unimportant decision.

Besides that, much of what happens in daily existence is stuff that simply occurs by chance without much influence of personal choice whatever. You're riding on a bus which skids on a turn and plunges off the road, killing scores of riders and injuring many more. Let's say you escape unharmed except for a few bruises. What part did your personal choice play in this scenario? Not much. You possibly could have made a different decision than taking this particular trip at this particular time on this particular bus, ad nauseam. But mostly what happened was simply a matter of chance. You were lucky to be alive and uninjured.

Think how often people in this sort of circumstance say, breathing a sigh of relief, "Someone was looking out for me." How about that! Apparently someone wasn't looking out for the ones that didn't make it. Does that mean that your guardian angel is a more vigilant angel than the ones guarding the other folks on the bus? I hardly think that'll wash.

The reality is that we live in a dangerous world that none of us will get out of alive. Things happen.

Some of them are really bad things. Sometimes we get lucky. Sometimes we don't.

When you couple this fact of life with the psychological reality that being blamed is not fun even a little bit, I guess it figures that people would welcome even the notion of angels who watch out for your welfare, as ridiculous as the idea is, rather than having to accept responsibility for what happens as a result of their own actions. And also, rather than having to acknowledge that chance plays a much bigger role in how things occur than it is comfortable for many people to admit.

So, as the title of this chapter says, I am decidedly UNTOUCHED by an angel. But don't feel bad for the angels.

Beings that don't exist don't have feelings.

A REALISTIC LOOK AT PRAYER

To pray or not to pray -- is that really a legitimate question?

The current controversies about offering spoken prayers in public situations, like gatherings of elected officials or classrooms or at compulsory military meetings, are symbolic of how ubiquitous the idea of prayer is in our society.

I feel confident that most church members have never thought about whether prayer makes any sense and/or does any good, and if so, why. I know I didn't as I was growing up. Everybody I knew "said grace" before every meal, as if the food couldn't be eaten without praying over it. Saying to someone, "I'll be praying for you" was *de rigeur*, almost like the virtually obligatory "Have a nice day" has become today.

But what is the purpose of prayer, and can the theory behind it be rationally justified?

The notion that human beings can make contact with a divine being by engaging in some kind of ritual behavior is as old as religion itself. In ancient times this ritual often included some sort of religious sacrifice, like the slaughter of a living human being or an animal or the burning of incense. The goal was to get the powerful deity to look favorably upon the petitioner.

I'm assuming that no intelligent human being in today's world would argue that offering sacrifices to get God on your side makes any sense. But in essence, that is what prayer is. Believers don't kill animals these days to please God, but they do bend their heads down (it's called "bowing in prayer"), close their eyes, sometimes kneel on the floor to symbolize abasement. In Islamic cultures, the faithful don't just kneel; they bend their whole bodies down until their heads touch the floor.

All this bodily posturing is supposed to indicate to the deity that one is appropriately humble, aware of one's unworthiness in the presence of divinity.

Then the spoken word, or prayer, is a plea for God to look favorably upon the person who is going through these contortions. Professional religionists go into great detail about the different kinds of prayers which may be offered -- the prayer of penitence, the prayer of thanksgiving, intercessory prayer, and many more -- but all of it boils down to one theoretical proposition, namely, that unless one engages in this exercise of trying to make contact with divinity, God won't be pleased with you, and bad things may happen.

There are several assumptions inherent in that idea. First, there is the assumption that God is in control of what happens in the world. That idea is supported by the language we use when natural calamities occur, which are commonly referred to as "acts of God."

Second, there is the assumption that God, if He chooses, can intervene in the natural order of things and change what would otherwise happen.

Third, there is the damaging assumption that unless faithful people pray, God either won't notice that something needs to be done or, even worse, won't care enough to intervene.

None of these assumptions will bear logical scrutiny. Let's examine them in order.

Take first the idea that some higher power is in charge of the world. There is overwhelming evidence that we live in a natural world, governed by natural sequences. Until relatively recently, as the universe measures time, humans had little understanding of what caused natural phenomena like volcanic eruptions, earthquakes, lightning, even rain. So primitive man came up with explanations for these natural occurrences which involved supernatural beings, or gods. We don't know the names of the earliest of such mythical supernatural beings, but we know some of the ways early man attempted to placate these beings. They were horrendous, but then early man had no way of knowing any better. Had we lived in those times, we wouldn't have known any better either.

But we know better now. We know that earthquakes are caused by the movements of our planet's tectonic plates. Earthquakes have happened on a regular basis for billions of years, ever since the earth began to cool enough for the tectonic plates to form. Similarly, volcanoes erupt because the pressure of molten rock beneath the earth's crust becomes too great to be contained, most often because of the converging or diverging of tectonic plates. We know that lightning occurs for natural reasons having to do with the discharge of positive and negative electrical energy within clouds.

Sometimes things like volcanic eruptions, earthquakes, and lightning strikes cause catastrophic consequences, but there is not a scintilla of evidence that these events are under the control of any super-being. They are simply natural events resulting from natural causes.

Likewise, many other life-destroying things occur in our world without deliberate human, or super-human, causation. Pestilence, plagues, droughts, floods, hurricanes, tornadoes, avalanches -- these regular occurrences chew up life and spit it out with no apparent concern for the pain and destruction being caused. It is simply the natural order of things.

Speaking of the natural order, think for a moment how heartless it really is, with some animals being born prey and some being born predators. The prey must live out all their days being constantly vigilant lest they become lunch, while the predators must live out all their days trying to be successful in killing something to eat or risk starvation. It is, quite literally, a heartless system with zero evidence that any caring being had a hand in designing it or managing it.

So let's turn to the second assumption behind prayer, that there is a God who can intervene in the natural order of things if He so chooses. Primitive human beings tried to discern a pattern for when and why natural occurrences like rain, volcanic eruptions, and drought occurred, and sometimes they noted an apparent connection between their own behavior and these events. Being scientifically naïve, as we would have been, too, had we lived in those times, they made unwarranted assumptions about these apparent connections. Thus were born superstitious rituals like the rain dance. Sometimes it did actually rain following a rain dance, and practitioners of such rituals would seize upon these times as proof that their incantations worked. They would, of course, totally ignore the many more times in which the same rituals were not followed by anything at all.

This kind of misreading of causal connections is called "anecdotal evidence", which simply means taking one occurrence of something as indicating a rule which can be counted on.

Think of the hundreds of times you've heard about someone praying for something which seemed unlikely, like the recovery of a loved one from a serious illness. Sometimes the person actually did recover in spite of medical predictions. These instances are taken by the faithful to mean that their prayers were effective and that without these prayers, the recovery wouldn't have happened. These are perfect examples of anecdotal evidence.

While we're at it, also think of how seldom you have heard faithful believers tell of times when they prayed diligently, and nothing happened. Somehow people of faith find ways to rationalize these times so that they can continue to believe that praying is a reasonable thing to do.

Recently I was in conversation with a very nice, intelligent person who disagreed with me on a certain issue. This particular issue had nothing to do with religion. I said I was interested in discussing it further with him and suggested that we have lunch sometime soon so I could hear more about his opinion and offer some reasons for my own view. He actually said, "I'll be happy to have lunch with you, John, but you need to know that I know what I believe, and no amount of facts will change my mind."

That's the way people who fervently believe in prayer are likely to respond to the whole subject of whether prayer is a useful activity. You may be aware that in recent years many empirical studies have been conducted, some well-designed, some not, to see if the benefits of prayer can be experimentally demonstrated. The usual design is to take a group of patients with similar diagnoses, like cardiovascular disease, divide them randomly into two groups, one group receiving regular prayer and the other one receiving no prayer. Well-designed studies are usually double-blind, meaning that neither the patients nor the caregivers are aware of who is in which group. Although a few studies have shown some minor difference in favor of the prayed-for patient group, which results have been ballyhooed to the skies by true believers, not a single one of these studies has been able to be replicated by other unbiased researchers.

The clear, empirical evidence is that prayer does absolutely nothing to induce some powerful, supernatural being to intervene in the natural order of things.

As Anne Nicol Gaylor, co-founder and President Emerita of the Freedom From Religion Foundation, is fond of asserting, "Nothing fails like prayer."

Dan Barker, former minister/evangelist who is now Co-President of FFRF, writes, ""If I got on an airplane and saw one of the pilots praying, I would get right off!" So would I, Dan. So would I.

The final, most damaging assumption behind the idea of prayer is that although there is a powerful God who is in charge of things and who can intervene in earthly affairs if He so chooses, He will either not notice that intervention is needed or simply choose not to do so -- UNLESS true believers grovel before Him and beg Him to get involved.

Remember, the Bible says, "Pray without ceasing." I can only take that to mean that if you only pray a little bit, it won't be enough to get God's attention.

To analyze why this assumption that unless you pray and pray really hard, God won't get involved, is so damning, let's use an analogy. God is referred to as Father, and human beings are his children. Suppose a six-year-old child has somehow wandered into a yard with a guard dog trained to protect the property. The dog, doing what it has been bred and trained to do, charges the child, knocks her down and is in the process of crushing the life out of her with powerful teeth and jaws. This is an imaginary scene, but we all know of instances when something like this has happened. The child screams in terror and pain. Her father comes out of the house next door, hears his daughter's screams and sees her plight, but his response is, "I don't think she has screamed loudly and long enough. I'll wait until she pleads with me some more before I decide to get involved. If she dies in the process of my making up my mind whether to respond, well, it just couldn't be helped. She should have been more sincere in her screams."

Can you imagine anything so absolutely abhorrent? How could any father worthy of the name be so utterly cruel?

Well, friends and neighbors, this is just what the theory behind prayer is suggesting. Throughout history multiplied millions of people have suffered horribly from all sorts of calamities without anything being done to alleviate the suffering. It would certainly seem that no one is in charge of what happens in the world on a daily basis.

Now I know you know, and I do too, that people of faith rationalize this horrible reality by saying that we aren't able to know just what God's ultimate purpose, or will, is. Leslie Weatherhead, the British minister whose book about Christian agnostics was helpful to me when I was still trying to be a believer, wrote an earlier book entitled **The Will of God** in which he tried to tackle this problem. He divided God's will up into three sections, one of which was God's permissive will. He tried to reason that there were certain things which God didn't really intend but that He allowed because of other factors which took precedence. Even at the time, that reasoning didn't hold water for me. Nice try, Dr. Weatherhead, but this effort is simply trying to justify the unjustifiable.

If we were only talking about minor annoyances, this might fly. But we're not. We're talking about indescribable suffering and death, all of which is a part of the natural universe we inhabit. Much of this agony results from natural events which have always occurred on this planet we inhabit. Some of this agony results from intentional damage done by other human beings. It is still going on in many parts of today's world.

Take your choice. Either there is a supreme being who is in charge of what goes on in the world, but He chooses not to intervene. Or,

NOBODY IS IN CHARGE.

The evidence is quite clear. Jesus is reported in Matthew 10:29 as saying that not even a sparrow falls to the ground without God's will, which idea prompted the popular gospel song "His Eye Is On The Sparrow", including the line that follows, "And I know He watches me." This prompts me to assert that if some powerful being is watching what's happening to the sparrows and to you and me, He's either not paying attention, incompetent, or incredibly heartless.

Or He doesn't exist. We're on our own. Instead of wasting our time praying for each other, we should get off our rumps and try to help make people's lives not quite so painful and empty.

REQUIEM FOR THE SOUL

If I were writing a funeral chant for the dead, which is what the word "requiem" in the title of this chapter literally means, I'd begin in my best monk-like monotone,

"O soul, thou who never wast and never wilt be,
We honor the idea of you, the intent of you,
The life-enriching meaning of you.
And we pledge our sacred honor to keep your essence.
But since thou art but figment,
Without pigment,
We herewith give solemn burial
To a concept most untenable,
And we sing humanity's freedom from your yoke.
We sing humanity's freedom from your yoke.
Amen.
And Amen."

All of which is to say that there is no such thing as

a soul. Not in the usual meaning of the word. The usual meaning, of course, is that each person has one which defines who the person is, that it has no physical referent, and that it allows the person whose spiritual essence it is to continue living beyond the grave.

The word "soul" in our language comes from an Old English word which meant essence or animating principle, but the concept is much, much older than the English language of whatever vintage. Indeed, the concept of soul probably dates back to the earliest Homo Sapiens who began to walk upright and philosophize about the meaning of life and death. If archeological evidence from ancient burial sites is on target, virtually all primitive peoples held to the premise that life in some form continued after death. Since the body obviously doesn't continue, it was necessary to assume that each person consisted of both a body, which dies, and a non-body, which continues to exist after life as we know it is over. This non-body, which nonetheless supposedly has a real existence, is what is meant by the common usage of the word "soul".

Given that the concept has such primordial roots in human history, it seems unlikely that any argument will be strong enough to get most people to re-evaluate whether there is such a thing as a soul. But on the off chance that you will give it a go, I offer this alternative way to think about "soul".

We begin with the pervasive desire of every person to believe that s/he has meaning beyond the protein and protoplasm that make up our bodies. And in fact, we do. Perhaps not in the unimaginably large scope of the universe, but within the framework in which we daily live and move and have our being, we most certainly do. Have meaning, that is.

To say that there is more to us as human beings than the mere molecules of which we're made up is incontrovertible. When a dear one has died, and you look at the lifeless body, don't you think, almost automatically, that the person you loved is no longer in this body? Of course you do. And you're right. The person you loved was much, much more than the tissue lying cold before you. Your loved one had a unique personality, a way of moving through the world, a style of interacting with you and others that, while not totally unrelated to her/his familiar physical attributes, was surely more than those attributes could explain.

I'm fairly sure this universal experience at the death of a loved one has occurred since earliest times. It is one of the two primary reasons the idea that humans have souls arose and became part and parcel of virtually all religions.

The problem is that there is another explanation which is more tenable, more logical, and which follows more heuristically from the evidence. To wit: the personality is a combination of thoughts, feelings, responses and patterns of behavior which emanate from the brain and its assorted nervous system synapses, some of which are whole body responses -- like anxiety or steely-eyed courage -- but all of which originate in the brain. It is clearly related to genetic inheritance, as well as personal history, which is why true identical twins not only look quite similar, but also have personalities which are very similar. It is also why people's personalities tend to be more like their parents and their siblings than most of us would like to admit.

If you alter the brain in a significant way, you have altered the personality. A neurological injury often leaves a person so different in style and behavior that it's hard to believe it is the same person. In fact, it isn't the same person. It is a different person. This fact is quite obvious when the brain injury has left the person in a vegetative state, but it is also true when the brain trauma has been less profound so that the person can still move about and function. The person you knew before the neurological injury has ceased to exist and has been replaced by this other person, with the degree of change dependent upon the extent and location of the damage to brain tissue.

But, someone insists, isn't it the same person really, with just some changes in manner? Of course not! Not unless the notion of personality were an essentially empty concept and did not mean that we can recognize a person not only by physical attributes, but by her/his pattern of actions, reactions, and interactions. When these change, it means you have a significantly different personality -- or essence of the person.

A dear friend of mine suffered brain injury in a sports accident. After months of critical medical condition, he slowly began to recover. His wife said to me after he had been home from the hospital for a year or so that he had apparently recovered all the functioning he was going to and that she estimated him to be approximately 60% back to normal. With deep emotion she said to me, "Although I'm so glad to have as much of him back as I do, I can't begin tell you how much I miss the other part of him that will never be back. It's like I'm living with a different person." Oh dear, dear friend, of course it's like that. Because you are.

Let's use, for another example of the same

phenomenon, the terrible, personality-altering disease of Alzheimer's. Many a caretaking loved one has said about the victim of this disease, "He is just not the same person as before this awful disease destroyed his mind." The brain had changed; therefore, the personality had changed; therefore, the person had changed. The person you knew and loved was no longer alive. S/he was dead, and a pale substitute of the person now inhabited the familiar body. Why? Because the brain had undergone profound changes.

You don't get this kind of profound change by altering any other part of the body. People who lose one of their senses (sight, hearing, etc.) don't become dramatically different people. The loss of a limb, while a terrible adjustment, doesn't change the person fundamentally. Nor does surgery to any area other than the brain, unless something goes wrong during the operation like lack of oxygen for too long, thus altering the brain permanently.

All scientifically rigorous (therefore, replicable) research on personality leads to this same conclusion. Let me restate it: the essence of the person resides in the brain. The rest of the body is involved in how this essence is expressed. But if you fundamentally alter the brain, you have altered the essence of the person. Ergo, if the concept of soul means the essential quality of the person that makes her/him unique, and if this expresses itself in what we call personality, when the brain is gone, the person is gone.

There is no soul, no essential part of us that goes on living after death.

Does the person live on in the memories of those who loved her? Absolutely. Some people even live on in stories told about them long after the people who knew them have died. Does some measure of the influence live on after death? Of course. For most of us regular folks, this is not terribly wide-spread or long-lasting, and it is discomfiting for us to have to acknowledge how quickly even the memory of us will pass into oblivion after we have breathed our last breath.

In fact, people in general have difficulty with the concept of ceasing to be, of non-being. It's a scary thought. Like going to sleep and never waking up, with no dreams to keep you company. Just nothing. If I'm brutally honest, I must admit that I cannot really imagine what that is like. Because everything I have known is based on the experience of being alive. However, I must also acknowledge that before I was born, I didn't exist. And it must have been okay because I have no memory of that non-existent state, good or bad. Still, there is something in us that wants to reject that idea and cling to the notion that we will continue to exist after death, just in some altered form.

We often use the fact that we have unique personalities to try to justify the idea that surely we cannot simply cease to exist. But if we use the argument that our very uniqueness insists that there must be some part of us (soul) that continues to exist after death, what about our beloved pets? They certainly have unique personalities, which are also related to brain function. Anybody who has lived closely with an animal as a pet and knows all of its idiosyncrasies and usual patterns of behavior knows that these precious animals have their own personalities, and that one is not interchangeable with another. What, apart from accepted religious doctrine, would suggest that we have souls (which are our essential personhood) but that these pets do not? Most animal pets don't talk human language. (I say "most" because we had a parakeet and a cockatiel who not only mimicked our language, but who clearly interacted with us on a conversational basis at times.) The fact that animals don't usually speak in words doesn't mean that that they don't communicate, both with each other and with us if we pay close enough attention to understand what they're saying. They think, they feel, they have unique individual personalities.

Some pet-lovers who have had to acknowledge how special and individual their pets are, but who hold to traditional beliefs about life after death, have decided that there must also be a doggy/kitty/cockatiel heaven to go along with the human heaven. Actually, one makes as much sense as the other. Which means neither one is likely to be accurate.

So the first of two primary reasons people cling to the idea of the existence of the soul is the unwillingness to give up the belief, based on zero evidence other than religious myth, that we somehow transcend our physical selves and continue to live on another plane of existence after the physical body has died.

The second reason is because of experiences that we label as "spiritual."

Most thoughtful people have had such "spiritual" experiences. In the traditional belief system, they are peculiar to religious observance and often occur in church. I certainly had many, many such experiences when I was a regular churchman, some of them after I began to think for myself and re-evaluate the theology I had been taught, although such experiences increasingly were independent of specific religious activities. The whole concept of worship is centered in the idea of a transcendent experience in which the human makes contact with the divine.

How do you know that you've had a transcendent experience? Because of the way it makes you FEEL.

That's it. Don't try to make it more complicated than that. What we call a spiritual experience is simply an emotional experience in a religious context or interpretation. This is why there is much more similarity between a rock concert and a fundamentalist revival than either bunch would be willing to admit. Both stir up the emotions within a group experience. The screaming teenager caught up in the fervor of a rock concert and the fervent believer, arms upraised and shouting "hallelujah" at a religious service are both experiencing the incredible high of a powerful emotional response.

In both cases, the experience is real. It's just that neither one is spiritual, neither dependent upon humans having a soul or spirit. You could say that both people, the rock kid and the true believer, are worshipping. I know that idea may offend you, but think about it. If the idea of worship involves suspending critical function and letting yourself be immersed in feelings engendered by the music and the ritual and the group assumptions/response, then worship takes place at both events. Do they have different consequences? Maybe. But psychologically they are indistinguishable.

Let me be clear. I'm not suggesting that what we call "spiritual" doesn't exist. It most assuredly exists, both in and out of religion, to say nothing of church services. But the experience of the "spiritual" is not dependent upon our having a spirit (or a soul) which is separate from the mortal part of us. It is, instead, dependent upon our being able to respond emotionally.

When the psychosurgery called "prefrontal lobotomy", which is commonly referred to simply as "lobotomy", used to be performed, it made for dramatic changes in personality and interactional style. The foremost portion of the frontal lobe of the brain was severed from the rest on the brain in this surgery, with the intent being to reduce behavioral problems related to hyper-emotionality. It often accomplished the purpose of calming the person, but at the horrendous cost of essentially destroying who the person was and might have been capable of becoming again. Such patients became emotional zombies, with flat affect and zero enjoyment of living. The fact that such surgery was still being performed, though rarely, in the mid-1900s is blatant testimony to how primitive our understanding of human psychological functioning still is.

I mention this horrible example of science stumbling its way to a better understanding of human functioning because my clinical experience with lobotomized patients is that they are completely and totally incapable of having a spiritual experience. The obvious reason is that they are incapable of feeling deep emotion. What we call spiritual is not inextricably tied in to our spirit (or soul), but rather it is inextricably tied in to our emotions.

Take away the emotional, and you take away the spiritual.

If you have followed the reasoning thus far, I want to assure you that it is inconsequential whether you choose to hold on to the word "spiritual" or the word "soul". Feel free to continue to use either of them if it pleases you. I still sometimes say that something thrills me to my very soul, even though I'm confident there is no such thing as a soul. I am only trying to help you see that having such experiences is not dependent upon there being such a thing as a human spirit, or soul. It IS dependent upon being able to respond emotionally.

A personal example may help here. I have always loved good music. Since I grew up in a minister's home and since all the members of our family were quite musical, I can't remember when I didn't know how to read and sing traditional Christian music. Long after I had to give up the traditional belief system in which I was raised because I could no longer believe it, I still enjoyed listening to and participating in good religious music. I play Handel's Messiah on my CD player and love nothing better than singing the bass solos or being in the chorus. As I write this, I am president of our local community chorale. At least half the music we perform is what is called "sacred" or religious music. And, I love singing it. Sometimes I feel such deep emotion when we sing that I tingle all the way down to my toes. There is a piece by Ralph Manuel called simply <u>Alleluia</u> that stirs me so profoundly I cannot begin to describe the feeling to you. There is only one word in the whole song, alleluia, and since nobody really knows what that means, I don't have to worry about text. And I am transported out of myself by the totality of the experience. If you were in the audience when we were performing that piece and watched me, you would swear I was having a spiritual experience. And in fact, I AM having what is usually called a spiritual experience. It's just that I know it has nothing to do with my having a spirit (soul), which I don't, and everything to do with my being deeply stirred by beautiful music.

I don't have a soul. But I have a brain which is capable of emotional response. And since I know that emotions are a good gift, but a poor guide, I simply revel in the gift, refusing to give up the power of the experience even though I know it is not actually transcendent. It is very earthly and animalistic, for animals also clearly experience emotions. We human animals probably have more opportunity to interpret our emotions than other animals do (I say "probably" because we really don't know for sure about that), but being able to experience emotions is a part of our animal heritage.

I know it is difficult to give up the idea that human beings have a soul. But once you do, if you do, you'll be surprised how little you'll miss it. It's an idea not supported by evidence or logic, an idea whose time has gone.

I propose we give it a decent burial.

THE BIBLE: IT AIN'T NECESSARILY SO

It "ain't" necessarily so.

It "ain't" at all divine.

And it sure "ain't" unequivocally good and edifying!

Since most garden variety church members in this country and in other "Christian" countries as well, have grown up with the notion that the Bible is a holy book, the "Word of God", and the guide for how we should live our lives in fidelity to truth, love, justice and all things good . . .

And since most of these sincere believers have either never actually read the Bible, or have read it quite selectively, or have read or listened to parts of it that are terrible by any standards with a mental filter that keeps them from acknowledging how horrible a given passage is . . .

And since unquestioned reverence for the Bible is promoted in our society by such things as placing a hand on it when swearing to tell the truth and by such common phrases as the "gospel truth". . .

The ideas I am proposing herein are sure to cause consternation within many people, even those who don't consider themselves strongly religious. The Bible as symbol for all that is holy and good is so commonly accepted in Western countries that to question that assumption is tantamount to, well, something outrageous like advocating selling your children into slavery.

But, as is true with many people who begin thinking for themselves and find that they can no longer agree with the basic tenets of religion, my rejection of religious faith came not from failing to read or understand the "good book", but from just the opposite -- spending half a lifetime reading it, memorizing it, trying to make sense of its inconsistencies and incongruities, studying the works of the most erudite Biblical scholars, fighting desperately to try to make my peace with the idea that even though the Bible is impossibly flawed, the basic truths of Christianity could still be worth holding on to, and finally, painfully, having to admit to myself and then in public that I could no longer be called a Christian.

There are many problems with considering the Bible a holy book, but I'm restricting this discussion to four major ones: the history of how it came to be in its present form, factual and scientific errors, internal inconsistencies, and the inhumane atrocities and horrible teachings of many of its passages.

Before I launch into this criticism, let me pause to acknowledge that in spite of all that is wrong with the Bible, there are indeed some beautiful passages and inspiring stories to be found within its pages. First Corinthians 13 is magnificent poetry about the primacy of love. Some parts of the Sermon on the Mount are a powerful reminder of how to keep life in perspective.

The Psalms contain passages with lovely metaphors in them. The book of Ecclesiastes, which was clearly written by a skeptic, approaches profundity in places. The story of Jesus standing up to the would-be stoners of the adulterous woman is a "profile in courage."

But there are few things useful or credible in the Bible that are not found elsewhere, and, on balance, rather than having the Bible enshrined in its current position in the western world as the unquestionable, unassailable holy book, civilization would have been better off had it never been written!

1. So let's turn to its history, how it was written and how it came to be in its present form. As most educated people know, there were many different writers over a period of hundreds of years, perhaps more than a millennium, whose work became a part of the Bible. Not only were the sixty-six different books which comprise the protestant Bible (the Roman Catholic Bible includes the "apocryphal" books as well) written by as many as fifty different people (the exact number is not certain), but many individual books which go by one name (Isaiah, for instance) had more than one author.

There is not a single original manuscript of any portion of the material in the Bible, and it is extremely unlikely any of them still exist and will be found. Even the earliest existing documents are copies of copies of copies. Painstakingly written out by hand with the primitive equivalent of quill and ink on parchment, by daylight or lamplight, mistakes too numerous to count crept in and were repeated in subsequent copies.

Not all the changes in text were accidental. There are numerous interpolations, phrases or passages inserted, that appear to be the result of intentional efforts by scribes to make the text conform to current accepted belief. A clear example is the story of Jesus' appearances to his followers in the last 12 verses of Mark. These verses were added long after the time when the story recorded in Mark was written in the first century. This is easy for Biblical scholars to determine because there are earlier copies which do not contain this passage. It was obviously added by a scribe who wanted the account to read the way tradition had been handed down, and the addition was subsequently recorded in later copies down through the centuries.

So how did the Bible come to exist in its present form? Hold on to your hats -- are you ready for this? -- it was voted upon. I kid you not. In plain English lots of different official (?) groups got together at various times over several hundred years to argue about, lobby for, and ultimately vote on what should be considered sacred scripture and what should not. Often there was nothing approaching consensus within these councils about whether a given book should be included in the sacred canon (the "official" listing of Bible books). It was just a matter of whoever could argue his (they were all males, by the way) case most convincingly and win the vote.

Does this sound to you like the way an omnipotent God would have chosen for his divine revelation to have been vouchsafed to humankind? By vote, for crying out loud!

To give you a small insight into how little the average believer knows about how the Bible came into its present form, let me tell you about a frequent comment that was made by uninformed churchmen when the first widespread modern version of the Bible, the Revised Standard Version, came out in 1952. Upset by any change in this "revered" book, fundamentalist preachers would say, "If the King James version was good enough for Paul and Silas, it's good enough for me!" The humor, and the pathos, in that statement is the lack of awareness that the Bible version they thought was the standard, original, "the-way-God-intended" one dates back to 1611, when King James I of England commissioned an official English version. This is where the archaic language with the "thou shalt" and the "verily, verily" came from. There's nothing sacred about the version or the language. That's just the way people talked in 17th century England.

To recap, the first reason the Bible is a flawed book is the history of how it came to be in its present form, including: no foggy idea of who most of its writers were, the fact that it was copied by hand over thousands of years with innumerable textual changes both accidental and intentional, and the process of professional religionists getting together in formal councils to vote on whether a given work should be considered sacred scripture or not. Not a very confidence-inspiring history, to say the least.

2. A second reason the Bible "ain't" necessarily so is that it contains a plethora of factual and scientific errors. Before I recite a partial list of the many dozens of places where the writers of the Bible had their facts wrong, let me say that they are not to blame for their inaccurate science. They were products of what was accepted scientific knowledge in their own time, just as we are. We know, for instance, that disease is not caused by demon-possession but by microbes, infections and viruses, and that many common maladies can be

avoided by higher standards of cleanliness and nutrition. But even 300 years ago when our forebears were colonists from Europe, such was not common knowledge.

However, since this book is touted as a divine revelation from the Almighty, who is commonly believed to be all-knowing, wouldn't you think this omniscient deity would have somehow managed to keep his human writer-vessels from perpetuating unfortunate and, in some cases, downright dangerous mistakes in scientific fact? It is incomprehensible to me that, if the Bible were really a revelation from God, it wouldn't be free from factual errors. And the fact that it has so many such errors leads me to the unavoidable conclusion that it can't possibly be divine in origin.

Here are some examples of Biblical errors in scientific fact:

<u>Noah and the flood</u> (Genesis 6-7). There is no archaeological record indicating a global flood ever occurred, nor is it possible one could have occurred. The amount of water available on the earth is constant, although the form changes constantly between solid, liquid, and vapor, and there is absolutely not enough water to cover the entire earth including all its mountain peaks. Almost all ancient civilizations have stories about huge floods; however, what they may have thought was the entire world was only their little section of it. Plus, the idea that any boat (ark) could have contained two of every species of animal on earth is ridiculous in the extreme. By the way, did it ever occur to true believers in the biblical story of the flood that if a supreme being wanted to wipe out all life on earth except for two of every kind of creature, why that

destruction didn't extend to the dwellers of the sea, including the air-breathing mammals like dolphins and whales, to say nothing of all the other sea life which greatly outnumbers all the land-based species on earth? The logical reality is that a worldwide flood never happened, scientifically couldn't have happened. Every serious biblical scholar knows that the first eleven chapters of Genesis are not history at all, but are mythology on the order of stories about Paul Bunyan or Odysseus.

Geocentric universe (Joshua 10:13-14). The Bible presents the sun as revolving around the earth, which enabled Joshua to command the sun to stand still while his army slew the Amorites. This scientifically inaccurate view held sway until Copernicus postulated in the sixteenth century that the earth revolved around the sun, not the other way around. In the next century Galileo's telescope confirmed Copernicus' theory, but he was imprisoned and threatened with death unless he recanted. Why? Because of the uncritical assumption that the Bible had to be right since it was the product of divine revelation and that scientific observations must be wrong.

Flat earth with domed heaven (Rev. 7:1, Acts 1:8, Romans 10:18) In keeping with the understanding of the times, Bible writers refer to the earth as having corners and an end, neither of which is possible on a sphere like the earth. Indeed, modern astronomy has not been able to discover any end to the entire universe, nor any corners. And the sky is most certainly not a solid domed structure with a heaven above it, from which a deity can open a window to pour down rain or blessings, or anything else. In fact, we know that the concepts of up and down are quite relative, that there is no such direction in the universe and that, for those of us who dwell on earth, up or down refer only to whether the direction is toward or away from our own planet. Our own astronauts have to quickly give up notions of up and down while circling the earth.

Impossibly young earth (Genesis 10-11) If one takes the genealogies of Genesis seriously, the entire universe is only a few thousand years old. One sincere churchman, Bishop Usher, added up the supposed years of human history and concluded that the earth had been created in 4004 B.C. Of course, it is fairly uncommon in today's world to find intelligent, educated believers who take this supposed tracing of human ancestry in the Bible literally. Nonetheless, the fact remains that the Bible purports to depict a creation history that is completely at odds with what scientific inquiry has revealed about the age of the universe.

Sexual reproduction as a divine curse (Genesis 3) Since the fundamentals of reproduction are very similar throughout the animal kingdom, it follows scientifically that human reproduction is the natural order of things, not that it was a curse placed on some female progenitor of the human race because of her disobedience of a divine prohibition. Likewise, the Biblical notion that female menstruation is the result of this curse and renders women unclean is totally at odds with human physiology.

Miraculous occurrences. The Bible is replete with reports of events that, if accurate, defy the natural order of things. Serpents don't talk, bushes don't burn without being consumed, seas don't pull apart leaving a pathway of dry land for people to cross, food doesn't fall from heaven, dead people don't rise up and walk, disembodied hands don't write on walls, people don't rise up and disappear into the skies. The list goes on and on. When someone reports something that doesn't happen in the natural order of things, the likeliest explanation is that the person who reported it is mistaken, or lying to gain some sort of advantage. Of course, another explanation is that a divine power contravened scientific laws in each of these specific instances, and you are free to accept that explanation if you choose, but it is intellectually, scientifically untenable. It is actually on the same order as believing in leprechauns or the tooth fairy.

3. A third reason the Bible cannot possibly be divine in origin is the fact, undeniable to anyone who takes the time to examine it closely, that it is filled with internal inconsistencies.

Essentially all reputable Biblical scholars, including those who continue to hold to some version of faith, acknowledge that many Bible stories and passages are at odds with other Bible stories and passages. They make their peace (rationalize?) with this fact by asserting that the Bible doesn't purport to be history, so that, in this view, the fact of disagreements between passages is irrelevant.

I tried to buy that explanation myself for many years while struggling to stay in the church and in the Christian ministry. So what if the Bible contradicts itself and, thus, clearly contains error. The fact that something isn't perfect doesn't mean it should be discarded. However, the overwhelming flaws in that argument finally wore me down, and I had to admit that to claim that the Bible is in some sense, any sense, divine revelation while looking head on at passages so contradictory that they can't both be accurate, is to stretch credulity to the breaking point.

The fact is that much of the Bible does purport to be history. What purpose would lists of genealogies in both Old and New Testaments possibly serve if not purporting to be factually, and thus historically, accurate? Nowhere does the Biblical text say, or even imply, that what is contained therein is mere fable or myth. It is fable and myth, of course, as any serious, unbiased analysis will reveal. A part of the evidence for that conclusion is the undeniable fact of the contradictions it contains. There are hundreds of such inconsistencies. We'll only look at a few, since to even list all of them would make this chapter much too long

Let's begin with inconsistencies in the very first Bible chapters, the creation story in Genesis. There are clearly two versions of this story. The first one in Genesis 1:1 - 2:3, and the second one beginning with Genesis 2:4 and continuing throughout the rest of chapter 2. In the first one the creator is shown making human beings on the sixth day, both male and female, after all the rest of creation had been formed, then resting on the seventh day. The second refers only to the "day that the Lord made the earth and the heavens", not six days, and gives the traditional story about making a man (Adam) first, then the animals that Adam was charged with naming, then noticing that Adam was all alone and taking a rib from his body to create a woman (Eve). Biblical scholars are clear that these stories were two different myths that were simply both included without trying to reconcile the two. It is obvious to me that if the Bible were really divinely inspired, this simply wouldn't have happened.

Likewise, the flood story has Noah instructed to take clean beasts (a stupid concept, by the way) into the ark by sevens (Genesis 7:2) and unclean beasts by twos. A few verses later (Genesis 7:9) Noah is said to have escorted all the beasts, fowls, creeping things into the ark by twos. The flood also is said to have lasted either forty days (Genesis 7:17) or one hundred and fifty days (Genesis 7:24, 8:3). Of course, no reputable Biblical scholar regards these early chapters of Genesis as accurate history. Indeed, they cannot possibly be history because of these (and many other) inconsistencies.

Moving to the story of Jesus, which is supposedly much more historically accurate than anything in the Old Testament, the genealogies contained in Matthew and Luke are significantly different. Both link Jesus' family tree through Joseph back to Abraham, with Luke going on with the linkage back to Adam. The lists of names are alike from Abraham to David, but it is totally different from David to Jesus. Here are the lists so you can see for yourself without having to wade through the biblical texts in Matthew 1 and Luke 3.

MATTHEW'S GENEALOGY	LUKE'S GENEALOGY
David	David
Solomon	Nathan
Roboam	Mattatha
Abia	Menan
Asa	Melea
Josaphat	Eliakim
Joram	Jonan
Ozias	Joseph
Joatham	Juda
Achaz	Simeon
Ezekias	Levi
Manasses	Matthat

Amon	Jorim
Josias	Eliezer
Jechonias	Jose
Salathiel	Er
Zorobabel	Elmodam
Abiud	Cosam
Eliakim	Addi
Azor	Melchi
Sadoc	Neri
Achim	Salathiel
Eliud	Zorobabel
Eleazar	Rhesa
Matthan	Joanna
Jacob	Juda
Joseph	Joseph
Jesus	Semei
	Mattathias
	Maath
	Magge
	Esli
	Naum
	Amos
	Mattathias
	Joseph
	Jana
	Melchi
	Levi
	Matthat
	Heli
	Joseph
	Jesus

As you can see Matthew's list contains 28 generations from David to Jesus, while Luke lists 43 generations, the only identical names being David, Joseph and Jesus. So which is it, 28 or 43? It can't be both. Even stranger, of course, about this whole subject is the fact that both Matthew and Luke claim that Joseph wasn't the biological father of Jesus, that feat having been accomplished by the Holy Spirit. Nonetheless the writers take great pains to show a lineage to Abraham through Joseph. Hmmm . . . For the true "Word of God", that sure seems an awfully foolish mistake about such an important subject!

The crucifixion story itself is quite different from one gospel report to the other. In all there were supposedly seven different utterances from Jesus' mouth as he was on the cross, but no account includes all seven. If this is so central to the Christian faith, wouldn't you think the almighty would have been sure the writers got it correct in each report? Human error? You betcha! Absolutely inspired truth in spite of the errors? Not likely.

Likewise the stories about discovering the empty tomb where Jesus' body had been laid vary significantly from one account to the other. Was the huge stone still covering the entrance when the women arrived as Matthew says, or was it already rolled away when the women arrived to anoint the body as the other three gospel accounts say? And how many angels (or men) explained about the resurrection? The accounts differ. Also to whom did the risen Jesus appear and did his body have substance so that he could eat real food and be touched or was it ethereal so that he could appear and disappear at will? There is no agreement in the accounts. Once again, this article of faith is so central to the Jesus story that it would seem imperative that the people writing about it in what would come to be considered the inspired "Word of God" would get the details accurate.

I have purposely only mentioned a few of the inconsistencies in the Christian Bible, but the implication of these inaccuracies is the same whether the number is in the hundreds, which it is, or whether it were only a few. A divinely-inspired record of such importance simply cannot have inaccuracies and still be considered valid.

4. Finally, let's consider the actual "teachings" of the Bible. Are they consistently morally uplifting so that the colloquial reference to the Bible as "the good book" makes sense? Hardly. Rather, it is filled with descriptions of inhumane atrocities and horrible teachings, all purportedly done or proclaimed in the name of God.

True believers talk about the Ten Commandments as if they were a blueprint for morality, and specifically a blueprint found only in Christianity. An essay in the next section will examine why that assumption is unwarranted.

But the Ten Commandments are not the only commandments, supposedly from God, that people are required to obey. There are countless other "commandments" in the Bible which any sane person would denounce as sadistic. For instance, in the same book in which the supposed "foundations of morality" (the Ten Commandments) were given, there is a commandment specifying that no person with a blemish (blind, lame, disfigured face, hunchback, dwarf, one long limb, etc.) can offer a sacrifice to the Lord. Such people must remain outside the holy place lest they offend the Almighty. How's that for equal treatment for those with disabilities!

In Exodus 21, immediately following the most familiar statement of the Ten Commandments (Exodus 20), there is an unsettling passage about what should happen if a man sells his daughter to another man as a slave. It says that she shall not go out as male slaves do, whatever that means, and then lists a bunch of possibilities about what may happen to her. All this with the tacit assumption that not only is it okay to have slaves (in this instance a sex slave), but it is also perfectly fine to sell one's own children into slavery! Now honestly, does that sound like divine inspiration to you?

Let me repeat: this horrible set of rules governing how one's children can be sold into slavery follows immediately after the passage that "true believers" say is the all-time most ethical set of commandments ever issued, the Ten Commandments. How thick do the blinders have to be for the faithful to ignore that blatant incongruity?

There are myriad commandments about what may and may not be eaten. Certain animals, birds, and sea creatures are arbitrarily designated "unclean" and may not be eaten. I shan't bore you with the long list, but it is found in the eleventh chapter of Leviticus. If someone so much as touches one of these creatures, he/she is considered "unclean" until going through a meticulously prescribed purification ceremony.

And while we're talking about the need for purification, the ritual demanded of women following childbirth and during and following their menses is particularly odious. It is very clear that the "Lord of the universe" is offended by afterbirth or menstrual blood. There is even a commandment about how long the mother is unclean following the birth of a son (seven days) as opposed to following the birth of a daughter (fourteen days). Go figure!

The penalties for violating one of these commandments range from extreme to horrendous. Things like slicing off a hand or plucking out an eye. A huge number of these proscriptions are followed by the insistence that the offender be killed. Here are a few of the offenses for which the death penalty is prescribed:

Being a witch or sorcerer -- Exodus 22:18

Having sex with an animal -- Exodus 22:19

Sacrificing to another god -- Exodus 22:20

Doing work on the Sabbath -- Exodus 31:15

Engaging in homosexual sex -- Leviticus 20:13

Cursing one's parents -- Leviticus 20:9, Exodus 21:17

Being raped without crying out loud enough -- Deuteronomy 22:23-4

Blaspheming the Lord's name -- Leviticus 24:16

Not only are the people of God instructed to summarily execute people who dare violate a commandment which supposedly came straight from God, the Biblical record is filled with senseless, indefensible slaughter of innocents at the behest of God. Much of this slaughter is in the service of the Biblical assumption that God decided, quite arbitrarily, to "choose" Abraham and his descendants to be his special people and that he "promised" them their own land.

Uhhh, 'scuse me, but there's a small problem with that promised gift; there were already people living on the real estate that God "promised" his special people, and they somehow thought it was their right to continue living there. (This is eerily similar to the "discovery" of America by Europeans and their assumption of the right to colonize it, never mind that there were lots of native people who had been living here for centuries before this continent was "discovered." Just move them out, or kill them, whichever comes first! Good Judeo-Christian principle, eh what?)

The Biblical story of how the Hebrews, God's "chosen people", were instructed to treat the indigenous people living in the part of the world that God supposedly gave them is almost too gruesome for words. I'll mention only a few examples, but there are dozens of such stories replete with horrible instructions supposedly from the Almighty about how the Israelites were to deal with the people living in the "promised land".

Exodus 23 makes it clear that God's "chosen people" are to completely take over all the land of Canaan and not allow any of the then current inhabitants to stay there. Deuteronomy 7 reports that God told them to show no mercy to the defeated people and to refuse to make a covenant with them (accept their surrender) even if they wanted to do so. God also supposedly said that if the defeated people tried to flee, he would send hornets after them until every one of them was dead.

Numbers 31 tells the story of what God's "chosen people" were instructed to do to the Midianites. They were to kill all the males, including old men and young male children, plus kill all the non-virgin women. But any young women who were still virgins should be divided among the conquering male warriors to be their "booty" (believe it or not, the Bible even uses that word to describe the human and non-human spoils of war)!

The story of Joshua who "fit the battle of Jericho",

as the quaint words of the familiar spiritual put it, is not quite so inspiring when you consider the actual details. After the walls came tumbling down, all the inhabitants were summarily executed with the "edge of the sword", including all their domestic animals, and all their belongings either burned or confiscated. The only exception was for Rahab, the harlot, who turned on her own people to help the spies who were sent ahead to scout out Jericho. No other exceptions means that all the elderly, all the infants, all the women and children were ripped open with swords.

Joshua celebrated this victory by issuing an oath which said that if anyone tried to rebuild Jericho, he would forfeit the lives of his first born son and his youngest son as well. This story is followed by tales of similar destruction of other nearby cities and all the inhabitants thereof. And at every point they glorify God for the massacres, claiming that their victories were because God so willed it. How does that square with the idea of doing the will of a deity who has just given them a commandment that "thou shalt not kill?" In light of that, doesn't the claim that the God who supposedly inspired the Judeo-Christian Bible "loves mercy and will do justice" seem just a mite hollow?!!

Then there are the "imprecatory" Psalms where horrendous fates are called down on the "enemies of God" (meaning those who had different religious views than the "chosen ones" of God). Horrible things like their teeth being ripped out, like falling into a pit and being buried alive, like pregnant women having their bellies ripped open, like mothers becoming widows whose children wander hungry in a hostile world. And the quintessential imprecation -- that the children of their enemies would have their brains bashed out against a stone. Try that passage from Psalm 137 as a bedtime story for your little ones!

Take the concept of hell. According to the Bible, hell is a place or condition of unremitting torment that never ends, reserved for all those who haven't believed the right way. Never mind how ethical, kind, or humane a person may have been, if he/she hasn't joined the ranks of the "saved", it's a lake of everlasting fire for the poor sucker. The teaching that we are all born in sin and, because of that fact, are deserving of eternal damnation is a bizarre notion. In essence it is saying that being born a human being, over which none of us had any control, by the way, is justification for an eternity of suffering.

If that isn't a horrible teaching, I don't know what is! And if you don't agree that it is a horribly unfair, atrocious notion, let me suggest you have simply not thought about it logically. It was the first of the teachings of religion I imbibed in my childhood that I found myself unable to accept once I began to think for myself. How could simply being born human be justification for an eternity of torment? Answer: it can't. The idea of hell is unconscionable. When I was in the ministry, I said from the pulpit that if there were a hell, I wanted to go there, because I didn't want to spend eternity with a supreme being who would create such a monstrous reality. Some of my parishioners gasped and feared that I had consigned myself to eternal damnation. I had, and have, no fear. There cannot possibly be such a place as hell, however much true believers who want to consign me there may wish it so.

I stand by my claim that the Bible is anything but a "good" book and that civilization would have been better off had it never been written. We will never know what the history of humanity would have been like had the Bible not been written and/or enshrined in Western culture as the inspired "Word of God". It's possible, I suppose, that the world would have been worse off or that some equally horrible book would have been given a place of transcendent honor in human affairs. And, of course, there are other books considered holy by other religions. I haven't spent a lifetime studying them as I have the Bible, so I won't presume to speak authoritatively about them. But from what experience I have had in reading from and about these other holy books (like the Book of Mormon, the Quran) I feel comfortable asserting that they are no more divine than the Bible and just as dangerous.

Enshrining a book as holy is simply a ridiculous thing to do. There are indeed some awe-inspiring things in the world, from the tiniest one-celled animal to the inconceivable infinity of the universe -- but an error-filled, scientifically inaccurate, impossibly-flawed book like the Bible is not one of them.

As I said, the Bible ain't necessarily so!

ESSAYS TOWARDS FURTHER LIGHT

The essays included in this chapter were all written as editorials for a local paper in Astoria, OR, where I was living at the time.

RETHINKING THE TEN COMMANDMENTS

A judge in Alabama has defied the law by insisting on posting the Ten Commandments in his courtroom. He reportedly believes very strongly that this set of rules from the Bible is the basis of societal morality.

He is not alone. Many a conscientious church member assumes that the Biblical Ten Commandments must be the definitive list about how people should behave. Included in that assumption is the uncritical acceptance of the Biblical story that these laws were handed down by God and that they were unique to the Hebrews.

There are problems with that assumption. A significant problem is that there is not just one version of the Ten Commandments recorded in the Bible. There are three, and none of them is precisely like the other two. For those who care to check this out, the locations are Exodus 20 and 34, and Deuteronomy 5. The first and third of these differ only in some wording, but the list in Exodus 34 is dramatically different from the other two. Interestingly, that list of commandments is the only place in the Bible where this set of laws is referred to as "ten commandments" and includes such precepts as being sure to observe the Feast of Weeks and not boiling a kid in its mother's milk, hardly the stuff of overarching morality.

Do you suppose God changed his mind about what should be included in the "big ten" between Moses' first and second trips up the mountain? Or that he couldn't remember what he'd said originally?

But suppose we overlook that incongruity and just accept the standard ten (for protestants) that are posted in the Alabama courtroom – and lots of other places, all illegal according to the First Amendment to the US Constitution, and all in King James English as if there is something holy about that archaic verbiage -- do these ten rules really include the most important precepts society needs in order to work well? Aren't there some significant omissions, as well as some questionable inclusions? Let's take a look.

The first four are purely sectarian – worship no God but Jehovah, make no images for use in religious observance, don't profane the name of God, and keep one day a week free from work so religion gets its due.

The first one clearly refers to the notion common to that day that each tribal group had its own god and that this particular tribe should remain true to its particular deity.

The second about no "graven images" seems designed to keep Jehovah as mystical as possible, and the punishment for violating it is obscene, namely that horrible consequences will be levied not only against the "graven-image" maker, but also against his children, grandchildren and great-grandchildren. Anyone who can defend that must be an expert in rationalization! How could any fair-minded person possibly think a just, not to mention "loving", deity would punish someone for the non-belief of his great-grandfather? Talk about petty!

Number three about not profaning God's name literally meant that they should never even speak the name aloud, once again an apparent attempt to keep a mysterious aura about the idea of their special deity.

And number four about keeping one day a week for religious observance was probably in the service of the religious professionals who were the ones most likely to benefit from such a system. It may, in fact, have other societal benefits, but it seems highly likely to me that this was the original intent of this rather shallow rule.

Number five says we should honor our parents, not a bad idea, but hardly one that could, or even should, always be insisted upon. Take, for example, the daughter whose father sexually abuses her on a regular basis and whose mother pretends not to notice because it lets her off the hook. Just what kind of honor would these parents be due, and if, upon reaching adulthood, the daughter managed to bestow honor upon such parents, how psychologically healthy would that be? Wouldn't you think emotional health would be better served by telling him what a sorry excuse for a father he had been and being sure to keep her own daughters from ever being alone with him?

The next four edicts, commandments six through nine, are more defensible. They are proscriptions against killing, committing adultery, stealing and lying. But it's important to note that these rules are not unique to the Hebrews or to their story in the Bible. Most other civilizations have operated on similar principles and have recorded them in their written codes. There is zero historical support for the idea that these rules wouldn't have existed without Moses' trip up Mt. Sinai.

And even these could stand some qualifications. Murder is, of course, wrong, but what about killing in self-defense or defense of another? If push came to shove, wouldn't you kill an attacker who was strangling your child and feel perfectly justified in doing so?

As for not engaging in adultery, which is generally harmful to a marriage or other committed relationship, this had the peculiar intent in Biblical times of being sure women were the private property of their husbands. Men were given considerable latitude. Surely there is a clearer way to talk about the improper use of sex.

And the commands not to steal and lie were only to be applied within the tribe. It was not only permissible to steal from a stranger; it was encouraged, as was deliberately deceiving him with lies.

The final commandment about not coveting has myriad problems, including the fact that it is useless to command people what to feel or not to feel, such as a longing that their lot should be as comfortable as their neighbor's. It also includes the assumption that it is okay to own slaves, which is what the terms "manservant" and "maidservant" mean in context. Not to mention the fact that this final commandment also conveniently lumps wives in with other male possessions, like his oxen and asses. On balance, the tenth commandment is worse than useless.

So I've come up with a new list of ten for your

consideration. I had some help from a discussion group which took on the project of trying to pare down all the possibilities to the most relevant ones. I make no claims that this list is definitive, and I don't think there is anything significant about keeping the number to ten. I only did so to try to show that, if you do restrict yourself to ten, there are some more essential things to mention than some of those in the Biblical Decalogue.

You, of course, may not agree with my list, and I would encourage you to try to come up with your own list of ten as a way of defining what you think is most important. I accept as a given that Biblical literalists will consider everything herein suggested as nothing short of blasphemy, but I can't let that deter me. And I suggest that you don't either.

So turn the page and read my list:

1. Make no claims regarding ultimate truth.

2. Never enslave another human being.

3. Do not commit rape, sexual violence, or any other sexual act (including consensual) between a competent adult and a child or incompetent adult.

4. Do no violence, except in self-defense or defense of another.

5. Be kind to all living beings under your care: children, the infirm, and animals.

6. Pass no laws restricting the acquisition of knowledge.

7. Never ridicule people trying to do their best, even if their best fails to meet your standards; save your ridicule for tyrants.

8. Do not knowingly cheat another person.

9. Be ready to help persons/animals in distress whose paths you cross.

10. Treat our planet and all its resources in a way that will allow all living things on earth to continue to call it home.

CLONING: ETHICAL DILEMMA OR RELIGIOUS CLAPTRAP?

Mary had a little lamb
Whose genes were cloned, you know.
And everywhere the story went
Nonsense was sure to go.
"It follows," said the grave and sage,
"They've broken God's clear rule."
What rule is that? Why, don't you know,
Only God can make a fool.

The news that scientists achieved a breakthrough in cloning a sheep named Dolly without benefit of a natural father has sent the world of moral guardians into a tailspin. From professor to priest, professional ethicists has raised a thunderous hue and cry across the land.

Today a sheep; tomorrow a human being. Think of the implications, they say. Well, by golly, why don't we do just that.

First, is this a genuine moral dilemma or only a religious one masquerading as ethics? What, pray tell, is unethical about reproducing a genetic replica of any living creature, human or otherwise? "Doesn't she have her mother's eyes," friends say about our newborn while we beam with pride. "Isn't he the spittin' image of his daddy!" All cloning will do is greatly increase the odds of success in an endeavor we've been about forever.

Second, could any reasonable person argue against replicating a Gandhi or a Mendelssohn, an Einstein or a Michelangelo? How wonderful if we only had a genetic replica of Socrates to apply his integrity and wisdom over such things as today's internet!

Ah, but what about a Hitler or a Jack the Ripper. Wait just a doggone minute. Banning cloning won't guarantee that there will never be another Hitler. Monstrous personalities are being created every day by the age-old method of sexual reproduction. Sometimes they result from the sexual union of two apparently normal people. Possible genetic combinations are virtually limitless, and occasionally genes do line up in unwelcome ways.

It can even be argued, since there are probably more well-meaning folks in the world than evil-intentioned ones, cloning just might eventually tip the balance towards sanity. At least, statistical predictions would say so. Besides, surely no one thinks there is a remote possibility that cloning will ever replace sexual conception. At best (or worst, depending upon your viewpoint) cloning would be only an adjunct to the standard process of peopling the planet.

No one knows how widespread human cloning will become and for what reasons, admirable or otherwise, it will be done. But there is nothing remotely unethical about it. Children would still be born to parents, and the only thing more complicated would be the legal issues around parentage. The **real** parents would still be the ones who filled the caregiver roles, who provided security and love.

When pictures appear on the TV screen of the two cloned Rhesus monkeys in Portland frantically clinging to each other for comfort, my ethical blood boils. Not because they were cloned by whatever method, but because they are obviously bewildered and terrified without a parent around for security. I have trouble believing that the research in which these little monkeys are involved could possibly justify the obvious panic that haunts the days of these precious and defenseless creatures. **This**, my friend, is an ethical issue, **not** the method of their conception.

What is unethical is treating any sentient being, human or not, like something to be exploited, as if only we humans have rights. God-given rights, religionists would add.

Ah, there's the rub. The real dilemma posed by Dolly and the implications of human cloning is solely and simply a religious one. Are we playing God? Will cloned humans have souls? Run, Chicken Little, run! The religious sky is falling!

This outcry over cloning is the modern day equivalent of the church's response to Copernicus' discovery in the 16th century that the earth revolved around the sun, not the other way around. It is the "How many angels can dance on the head of a pin?" question for our day.

And it is just as silly.

FREEDOM FROM FANATICAL FAITH

Perhaps the most frequent comment in the aftermath of the terrorist attacks on the World Trade Center and Pentagon has been, "Things will never be the same again."

What will be different? Our sense of invulnerability as the world's most powerful country? Certainly. Our feeling of safety within our own borders? Probably. Our ability to be aware at all times of the preciousness of life and of its frightening fragility? Hopefully.

There is something else that I wish could change -- the assumption that religious faith is always a good thing. I have no illusions that this change will, in fact, happen because cultural acceptance of religious ideation is so incredibly strong. But as Martin Luther said when he nailed his ninety-five theses to the door of the church in Wittenberg, thus beginning the Protestant Reformation, "Here I stand. I cannot do otherwise."

Since it seems clear that the atrocity of September 11 was plotted and funded by the group of rabid Islamic fundamentalists led by Usama Bin Laden, let's examine what underlies a movement like his. The foundation of such movements is fanatical religious faith. In this instance, a perversion of the primary tenets of Islamic faith, perhaps, but religious faith nonetheless. Ironically, the U.S. helped arm his group when he joined the Afghans in fighting the Soviets with whom we were engaged in a cold war at the time. He turned against our country during the Gulf War because he said we were violating sacred ground by placing our troops in Saudi Arabia.

Note the word "sacred", a religious concept, not a

political one. He now talks openly about America as an evil nation (again, a religious notion) and instructs his followers that they are doing the work of God (Allah to Muslims) when they kill Americans.

But by far the most telling evidence that this attack was the result of religious fanaticism is the fact that it involved suicide bombings. People seldom are willing to volunteer for suicide missions for purely political reasons. But for religious reasons? Ah, yes. Tragically, yes. Especially when their religious leaders promise them that the result of their sacrificial suicide will be instantaneous access to the highest of heavenly rewards.

How could any intelligent person believe that? Because it is a matter of faith, not reason. Faith is, by definition, non-rational. That doesn't necessarily mean it is irrational, although it certainly may be. Mark Twain's famous quote is that "faith is believing what you know ain't so." Twain may have been overstating the case to make a point, but in reality faith is accepting what cannot be logically or empirically supported. (I am deliberately not using the word "proved" because neither logic nor science can ever "prove" anything, only find or fail to find support for a given proposition.)

Those believers who claim otherwise, that they know for certain that their belief is true, are making an emotional statement, not a logical one. To demonstrate, consider this pertinent question: Do most Americans believe that these suicide bombers went immediately to the highest heavenly reward? Surely not, because this is not what their faith teaches. But it is what the faith of the suicide bombers teaches, and you can bet that they were 100% convinced that they were correct. In a horrible play on words, one could say that this attack was the ultimate "faith-based" initiative.

Lest you think that such fanatical faith is only found in non-Judeo/Christian traditions, let me remind you of the tragic stories of Jim Jones, David Koresh, the Heaven's Gate cult, and, if we go further back in history, of the atrocities committed by faith-based movements like the Crusades, the Inquisition, and the Salem witch trials. These horrific expressions of religious fervor were fueled by the unquestioning conviction that they were doing the work of God. And remember that Hitler claimed his horrible attempt at world domination and elimination of the Jews was based on religious convictions, however misguided.

Which brings me to the crux of the matter: what needs to be different in America following the tragic consequences of these terrorist attacks is that we need to be wary of those who are convinced that they and they alone have the ultimate truth. That is the essence of religious fundamentalism, whether Christian, Islamic, Judaic, or virtually any other religion. Fundamentalist faith is almost always based in the belief that they have access to a divinely-given document that is the final word and cannot be questioned, like the Bible, Koran, Torah, or Book of Mormon. It also usually involves the belief that they have direct personal access to God and that their lives are being divinely guided.

Such people have been, are, and will be again quite dangerous. Not all of them, of course, because most are relatively benign even in their certainty that they are the only ones who know ultimate truth.

Does this mean that I'm suggesting that all religion

is inherently dangerous? Not necessarily, although I am dismayed by how little most believers know about why they believe what they believe. I personally, as a matter of integrity, am no longer able to be a member of a traditional religious group, although I was raised in the church by a Southern Baptist minister father and spent many years of my young adult life as an ordained minister. I still know hundreds of ministers personally and thousands of devout church people whom I am pleased to call friends. Most of the church members are sincere and wonderful people, big-hearted, loving, kind. And many of the ministers genuinely try to do good in the world, although the better educated ones know that the theology they proclaim is highly suspect. Nonetheless, they are trying to make the world a better place, and I applaud them.

I also join them when I can. I love singing Handel's MESSIAH and Vivaldi's GLORIA. I have sung in the choirs of many local churches because I love good music, including good religious music, even though I am unable to accept the theology on which it is based.

But I cringe at the mistaken notion that America was founded as a Christian nation. It wasn't. It was, instead, founded as a secular nation in which the likes of Thomas Jefferson and James Madison made sure that people would be free to practice any religion they chose. Or no religion!

We are one world, with people of many faiths, and no faith. To the extent that your belief system helps you be more accepting of others, more generous, more loving, I honor your faith of whatever variety. And I will join you in praying for a better world following this tragedy, although I'm convinced that the only value in prayer is in what happens inside the person, not in persuading any deity to intervene. I also don't think there was any divine purpose in this atrocity, only the twisted purpose of the religious fanatics who perpetrated it. The idea that a loving God would deliberately allow such a thing to happen in order to teach his children a lesson is too sick for words.

I conclude with noting an intriguing incongruity in language usage following the tragedy. The president proclaimed a day of prayer and remembrance. While that was being announced on television, a printed message from House Speaker Dennis Hastert was crossing on the bottom of the screen, which said, "Osama Bin Laden had better say his prayers!"

Hmmm. Same word, prayer, with one usage a call to piety and the other a warning of revenge. I suppose there are prayers and then there are prayers.

What we need to watch out for is fanatical faith.

FAITH-BASED INIATIATIVE A BAD IDEA

The current administration's proposed legislation to grant money from federal tax coffers to "faith-based organizations" to help provide services to various needy groups should be studied carefully . . . and then voted down! Unless in the unlikeliest of outcomes there is some way to guarantee absolutely that none of this tax money would be used for religious indoctrination, either actual or implied.

I cannot imagine how such a guarantee could be made -- or policed.

It is not that I am against the activity of churches and other faith-based groups in remediating human suffering. Quite the contrary. I wish a much larger percentage of the budget of religious groups were invested in such "good Samaritan" activities instead of in the usual "pad the pews" kind of expenditure. More power to the many church programs that are designed to help those in need.

My concern is that we must be "Simon pure" in our respect of the separation of church and state that the founding fathers wisely wrote into our constitution. Jefferson and Madison were quite clear that state-sponsored religion leads to incredible abuse of individual freedom of conscience, a *sine qua non* of the Land of the Free.

Joe Lieberman's reported statement during the recent presidential campaign that "freedom OF religion doesn't mean freedom FROM religion" is dead wrong. It means both or either.

Although many of the early European settlers of this continent were motivated by the desire to flee religious persecution, they were not always careful, once having gained freedom for themselves, to allow others to dissent from their own religious views. But by the time of the American Revolution and the subsequent drafting of the Constitution, it was clear to the framers that all faiths should be allowed and respected and that none should be officially promoted or sponsored.

The path of granting tax money to religious organizations is a slippery slope, however well-intentioned the proposal. Funds in most such organizations are fungible, meaning that money used in one activity is interchangeable with money used in another activity. It is easy to see how $1000 of tax money for a non-sectarian part of a program frees up a similar $1000 from adherents for the religious aspect of a program, effectively subsidizing the religious contributions with tax dollars.

Further worries from some religious leaders also deserve careful attention. Such as the possibility (likelihood?) that with federal dollars comes federal control, a quick way to dilute the essential elements of such programs. Another potential outcome stems from a predictable psychological phenomenon, namely that when easy (read that "from the tax coffers") money appears on the horizon, charitable giving by members and adherents tends to dwindle. The idea that "if the government is going to do it, I don't need to deprive myself to make it happen" is as old as organized government itself.

Another concern, raised on many recent TV programs on this issue, is whether fringe religious movements, like Louis Farrakhan's group which endorses racial enmity or Ron Hubbard's Scientology movement which has a ton of philosophical ambiguities, would be included. The answer was given that if a group preached hate, it wouldn't be included. But who makes those decisions? And is it smart to grant that kind of power to fallible human beings with their own biases and agendas? Hardly!

There is no disputing the evidence that many faith-based programs have generated outstanding results. Whether these results are actually due to the underlying philosophy of the group sponsoring the program (as opposed to the fact that somebody seems to care and that participants begin to really believe things can be better) is immaterial. So long as the programs are entirely voluntary and the money used to support them is entirely voluntary, it essentially doesn't matter WHY a given program works, only THAT it works.

But the dangers of beginning to subsidize with tax dollars humanitarian programs that have a religious belief system central to their method and mission are very real. The time in recent human history when religion and government were inextricably entwined is not referred to as the Dark Ages for nothing. When a scientist like Galileo, whose telescopic sightings supported Copernicus' theory that the earth revolved around the sun, was placed under house arrest for the last eight years of his life because his scientific opinions were not consonant with accepted religious belief, this began to signal the end of such a dark period. But a return to such insistence on religiously "correct" positions is not totally unthinkable. Consider what happened in Iran and Afghanistan in recent years when the dominant religion came to power.

Religious belief, or lack of it, must, I repeat MUST, remain a private matter with no sanctioned government support or involvement whatsoever.

Religious humanitarian programs are alive and

well. May their tribe increase. But let's tell the government thanks, but no thanks. And let's keep trying to make life better for as many people as we can, whether such efforts are motivated by religious doctrine or just simple human caring.

INTEGRITY VERSUS IDEOLOGY

The huge challenge confronting modern civilization, staring at us with the war-weary eyes of the ghost of errors past, is how to replace ideology with genuine respect for reason.

Make no mistake; terrorism is fueled by ideology, most of it religious. You don't defeat deeply-held ideology by using overwhelming force, as the 50-year battle between Israel and Palestine attests.

Ideologies are essentially belief systems, which, by definition, are notoriously absent of replicable evidence. They are typically learned early or born of internal experience and spread by hearsay. The hearsay may be what some people call a holy book.

To use an incontrovertible example, prior to Copernicus the common wisdom was that the earth was the center of the universe, with the sun revolving around it. Essentially everyone in the Western world was convinced that this was reality, with the Bible being the main evidentiary source. But Copernicus, although devoutly religious, was open to evidence, even if it contradicted "Holy Scripture," for which he was roundly condemned by the church.

All legitimate scientists follow where replicable evidence leads, and, indeed, most intelligent, well-educated people tend to do so as well. In the matter of ideology versus intellectual integrity, we need to advance to where integrity wins hands down.

Civilized countries ought never to prescribe what people's belief system should be. People should be able to believe any damn thing they want to believe so long as it doesn't hurt others or infringe on their freedom -- and so long as it isn't supported by public monies.

The life-and-death challenge we face is to somehow

keep competing belief systems from blowing the world apart until we can get enough of the world's population educated to the place that they are open to evidence, rather than bound by ideology.

I'm afraid that the world may not last that long, not because some god decided to destroy it, but because in the name of some god we've done the job ourselves.

TIME FOR REAL MEN TO STEP FORWARD

I am an unabashed feminist.

I didn't start out life a feminist. In fact, my youthful views would probably have qualified me for a male chauvinist button. Not that I didn't dearly love the company of the opposite sex once puberty had arrived. I just had no idea what a leg up I had received simply by being born male.

But I matured and became a feminist when I saw what the world is really like, including for my own daughters. I look forward to the day when the term feminist is an anachronism because it is no longer needed. But that day is, lamentably, not yet on the horizon, at least not one I can see.

What brings me to the need to hype the women's movement at this juncture is a recent column by Eileen McNamara of the Boston Globe about a Web site called wife- beaters. This Dallas, Texas, business is selling tank tops on-line with this term emblazoned on it. For an extra dollar you can get one with a simulated blood stain. There are even wife-beater shirts for toddlers, presumably of the masculine gender.

This sick site is accompanied by music (?) by a group called Prodigy singing lyrics that say, "Smack my wife up, shack my wife up, smack my wife up." As a further strain on credulity, if a customer offers proof of conviction of domestic violence, he can get a second shirt for half price. The site is plastered with pictures of a man spanking the bare bottom of a laughing woman.

But this is no laughing matter. The FBI reports that every year in this country over two million women are beaten by the men in their lives. Many of them either stay with or go back to these men, often for economic reasons. Simply put, they are afraid they can't make it on their own, especially if they have children who still need care. Plus, they may truly be terrified for their lives, since statistics indicate that women who get the courage to leave abusing men are actually in more danger of being killed than those who stay and get beaten.

And this is in the USA, which we like to think is one of the more progressive countries in the world. Think of what the plight of women is like in countries like Afghanistan. Since the ultra-conservative Muslim movement called the Taliban took over this country in 1996, Afghan women have suffered unbelievable reprisals. Women may not appear outside their houses without being totally covered head to toe by a garment called a burka, may not go anywhere unless accompanied by a male relative, may not see a male doctor (and female doctors are now forbidden, as are all professional positions for women), and may be publicly beaten or even killed for violating any of these restrictions.

A most disturbing development is that the US has now entered into an alliance with the Taliban government in Kabul to halt growing of opium poppies, granting this government by religious fanatics $43 million to make such farming illegal on religious grounds. Since the country is facing economic ruin because of other policies initiated by the theocratic rulers, so that adequate infrastructure for crops like wheat or corn is lacking, this money is hardly a down payment on what will be needed in the future if we are to continue shoring up their failing economy.

But the shameful import of this Faustian deal is that it points up that we care more about winning the war on drugs than about half the Afghan population who live with oppression virtually indistinguishable from slavery. *(This editorial was written several years before the 9/11 attack and our subsequent war in Afghanistan.)*

Or take the fact that in much of Africa and Eastern Europe women, particularly young women, are still regularly kidnapped, sold, and traded into actual slavery, sex slavery. The State Department estimates that as many as 100,000 young women and girls are smuggled into the US each year into sexual bondage, some under the guise of "mail order marriages." Annual trafficking in the sex slave business may be as high as 12 billion dollars, according to the International Organization for Migration. When these cases are discovered, the women are often treated as criminals rather than victims and frequently deported without being allowed to testify against their enslavers. So the penalties for the traffickers in human bondage are either non-existent or light.

I don't know where the lowlifes who engage in this sort of despicable enterprise make their home, probably not in Clatsop County. But I do know that we have our share of domestic violence in our area. Although such violence occurs across the entire socio-economic spectrum, the most likely perpetrators are probably not reading this column. What perplexes me is the fact that more women, all women in fact, aren't openly distressed. I have an intellectual understanding. The phenomenon is referred to in psychological terms as "identifying with the aggressor", a defense mechanism exemplified by the Patty Hurst kidnapping case when she became Tanya the bank robber.

And I also understand how that can happen. When

people are trying desperately to keep from drowning, they are most reluctant to rock the boat.

So my plea is to the real men in our midst, the ones who don't have to hide behind macho posturing and false symbols of masculinity like a t-shirt that boasts of beating the person you claim to love, to step forward. Let your voice be heard. Join me in openly declaring that you have grown out of your juvenile need to feel superior to women and become an unabashed feminist.

It is true that women in this part of the world have come a long way since the days when they couldn't even vote or own property, which hasn't been all that long ago, by the way.

But until a Web site like the sick one that motivated this column is not viable because our society has outgrown the immaturity it bespeaks and the real obscenity it portrays, we must continue to speak out. Particularly the real men among us. The ones who are not ashamed to be known as feminists.

Are you familiar with the powerful piece written by Martin Niemoeller, a protestant minister in Nazi Germany? "First they came for the Communists, but I was not a Communist so I did not speak out. Then they came for the Socialists and the Trade Unionists, but I was neither, so I did not speak out. Then they came for the Jews, but I was not a Jew so I did not speak out. And when they came for me, there was no one left to speak out for me."

EPILOGUE

I have tried to lay out the reasons that I essentially had no choice but to outgrow religion.

It is not something I wanted to do. Quite the contrary. Except for my ever-increasing theological quandary, I was most comfortable in the church, and I had no trouble filling the role expected of me as a minister. I loved being there to try to help people through life's painful times, to rejoice with them in their celebrations, like a wedding ceremony or the birth of a baby, and to try to console them in their losses.

The church was family to me. It was where my friends were. It was where my life was.

It WAS my life.

I understand perfectly well why people, even otherwise intelligent people who value science and evidence and reason, find it more than a little difficult to allow themselves to even consider "outgrowing" religion.

Plus, besides the fact that the local church congregation is, for many of its members, a comfortable extended family, there is religion's powerful pull of assuring believers that someone all-powerful, all-wise, and all-loving is in charge of what happens in our chaotic world. Religion even assures that this supernatural being has a plan for the life of each individual person and that all one has to do is submit oneself to finding and following that plan – and all will be well.

However, there is no credible evidence that this is the case. The "holy books" that supposedly tell the story of the supernatural are clearly not even close to being of divine origin. There have been countless philosophers/thinkers/teachers down through the centuries who have pointed out much more helpful pathways for how to live one's life in a meaningful way than all the "holy books" combined.

I understand, also, how powerful a supposedly spiritual experience can be. As I pointed out, it is not actually a "spiritual" experience at all, since there is no evidence anyone possesses a spirit or soul, only a brain which is part of the physical body. What has happened to people who claim to have been "born again" or to be "filled with the Holy Spirit" is that they have had a powerful **emotional** experience which has been filtered through their religious belief system. I'm not knocking the power of such an experience. It is for many people quite real. I'm just saying that there is nothing mysterious or supernatural about it.

I also want to reiterate that I am happy to acknowledge the good that religious organizations (like churches, synagogues, mosques) have done, and are doing. For every religious group which feeds the hungry, clothes the naked, houses the homeless, in general tries to take care of the "least among us", I rejoice. I wish a much larger proportion of the financial resources which religion takes in would go to such endeavors, but nevertheless, I applaud all the good that is, in fact, done in the name of religion.

I have tried to explain in this book why thoughtful, inquiring minds may very well find it difficult to continue to believe in the basic tenets of their religion once they have begun to evaluate the realities of how it all began and how it came to be handed down to them as a package, take it or leave it. Just as no sensible person would continue to believe in Santa Claus, or the Easter bunny, or the tooth fairy – or in leprechauns, satyrs, mermaids, centaurs and other mythical creatures like angels or demons – sensible people should consider giving themselves permission to question whether they believe in an actual virgin birth, or a bodily resurrected Jesus, or a "holy ghost", or an afterlife of eternal bliss or torture.

People certainly have every right to continue to believe whatever their particular religion has taught them to believe. I frequently told my psychotherapy patients, if your belief system really gives you a genuine sense of life satisfaction, stick with it.

On the other hand, if you are experiencing significant questions about your inherited religion (over 90 per cent of religious affiliation is the product of the community in which its adherents were raised), and if you, like me, simply cannot reconcile what you have been taught with what actually makes sense, then I hope you will consider allowing yourself to "outgrow religion."

That most assuredly doesn't mean you have to outgrow your sense of morality, though reason may require you to modify what you decide is actually immoral, or of living your life with a sense of purpose and integrity. My contacts with the secular humanist community since leaving organized religion leads me to conclude that humanists are certainly no less moral than the typical person of faith.

I mentioned that the British minister Leslie Weatherhead suggested in his book <u>The Christian Agnostic</u> that a person of faith should accept only those aspects of theology which have validated themselves in his/her own experience and that all other claims should be put in a mental drawer labeled "awaiting further light." I am convinced that "further light" has indeed been forthcoming for me once I allowed myself to be influenced by evidence that makes sense, not by tradition that doesn't.

Entitling this book "Towards the Light" is an accurate description of my path from being a fifth-generation Baptist minister to being a secular humanist (atheist, if you please, but not an angry one) who rejects the whole idea of the supernatural in favor of science, reason, and being good for goodness sake.

Outgrowing religion has been a long, difficult, and sometimes painful process for me. It has also been unbelievably freeing.

Being good for goodness sake is a great way to live your life!

I covet that same freeing experience for every believer.

AUTHOR BIOGRAPHY

John S. Compere, PhD, is a retired Licensed Clinical Psychologist and Professional Speaker who currently lives in Chandler, Arizona, with his wife, Joyce.

Dr. Compere received a BA in English from Mississippi College (1956), a BD in theology from Southeastern Baptist Theological Seminary (1961), an MA in psychology from Wake Forest University (1969) and a PhD in clinical psychology from the University of North Carolina (1972) and subsequently taught psychology at Wake Forest University and Medical School in Winston-Salem, NC, as well as having a private practice as a clinician. He was a member of the American Psychological Association, the American Association for Marriage and Family Therapy, and the American Association of Sex Educators, Counselors, and Therapists. He also was one of the initial consultants at the Center for Creative Leadership, Greensboro, NC, and from that association began speaking to corporate and professional conferences on Psychology You Can USE. He became a full-time professional speaker in 1989 and has spoken in 48 of the 50 states in the USA. He was a member of the National Speakers Association and served as the President of the Carolinas Speakers

Association while living in North Carolina. He is currently a member of the Freedom From Religion Foundation, the American Humanist Association, the Humanist Society of Greater Phoenix, and of Americans United For Separation of Church and State.

Prior to going back to graduate school in psychology, Dr. Compere was a Southern Baptist minister, having been ordained at 18 as the fifth-generation in his family of Baptist ministers. His great, great grandfather came to America as a missionary from the London Missionary Society, working with Native Americans. John also served as a student missionary to Alaska on two different occasions during his teens, living and building a church building in the small Eskimo village of Selawick, AK. Including student pastorates while in college, he served four different churches as pastor, as well as serving as youth minister at the campus church while in seminary.

John's doubts and concerns about the authenticity of the tenets of the faith he had inherited began in college and finally culminated in his leaving the ministry at age 32 to go back to graduate school.

John's wife Joyce is a retired special education teacher, the former co-owner of an auto racetrack, and most recently the Executive Director of the Astoria Sunday Market. John and Joyce enjoy cycling, live theater, classical music, racquetball, hiking, and taking long car trips together while discussing political and philosophical issues. Joyce refers to herself as a "recovering Catholic" and shares John's views on outgrowing religion. Between them they have four children from former marriages and six grandchildren.

Breinigsville, PA USA
04 October 2010
246674BV00002B/1/P